INTERFACT REFERENCE

THE BOOK AND CD-ROM   THAT WORK TOGETHER

ATLAS

World Book

What's in the book?

What's on the disc?

First, get your Interfact passport. Follow the instructions on screen. Then explore the interactive maps and use the Picture Index to discover fascinating facts about the world's animals, plants, peoples, and places. As you travel the globe, be sure to visit the capital cities—some of them feature fun activities and exciting adventures (see right).

There are 16 interactive maps to explore.

Installing the Atlas CD-ROM

See page 48 for troubleshooting tips, system requirements, and helpline details.

Windows 95 or 98
The Atlas program should start automatically when you put the CD into your CD-ROM drive. If it does not, follow these instructions:
1. Put the CD into the CD drive
2. Double click on My Computer
3. Double click on the CD drive icon
4. Double click on the **Atlas** icon

Windows 3.1 or 3.11
1. Put the CD into the CD drive
2. Open File Manager
3. Double click on the CD drive icon
4. Double click on the **Atlas** icon

Macintosh
1. Put the CD into the CD drive
2. Double click on the **Atlas for Mac** icon

Power Macintosh
1. Put the CD into the CD drive
2. Double click on the **Atlas for Power Mac** icon

Virtual Globe

Take a closer look at the world using an amazing 3-D globe and answer rapid-fire questions on the continents.
Location: Sydney

Find Agatha

Track down your long-lost Aunt Agatha using the book to solve the clues in the postcards she sends you.
Location: Washington, D.C.

World Class

Find the answers to all your questions about mapmaking and geography—this teacher is in a class of her own!
Location: Brasilia

Jigsaw Map

Pick up the pieces and put the world back together with these interactive jigsaws. Once each jigsaw is finished, click away to find out more!
Location: Tokyo

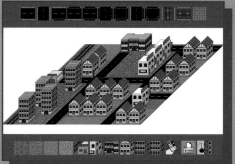

Map Maker

Create your own maps on screen. Print them out to keep or put your map-reading skills to the test and help Agatha find her missing purse.
Location: Cairo

Picture Index

There are over 400 interesting pictures in your Atlas. Use the Picture Index to find out more about each one—from Antarctic cod to desert lizards!
Location: Toolbar

*T*he Toolbar

The toolbar appears whenever you move the cursor to the right-hand edge of the screen.

 Click here to return to the main screen.

 Click here to go to the Picture Index.

 Click here to see activities completed.

 Click here to see your passport.

 Click here to use the note pad.

 Click here to go to the gift shop.

 Click here for help.

Click here to quit.

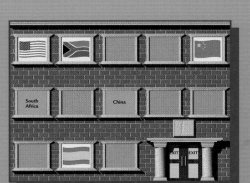

Windows on the World

A crazy memory challenge to test your knowledge. You'll be racing against the clock to match up countries with their capital cities, currencies, languages, and flags!
Location: Moscow

Around the World in 80 Days

Help Phileas and Passepartout navigate their way around the world. Visit more than 150 capital cities along the way.
Location: London

What is an atlas?

An atlas is a book of maps showing different parts of the world. Maps are small pictures of big places drawn from above. They can show somewhere as small as a village or as big as the world. You can use atlases and maps in all sorts of ways. They might show you how to find your way around, or tell you what a place is like.

1 One of the most difficult maps to draw is one showing all of the world. This is because the world is round, like a huge ball, but maps are flat. Imagine painting the world onto the skin of an orange.

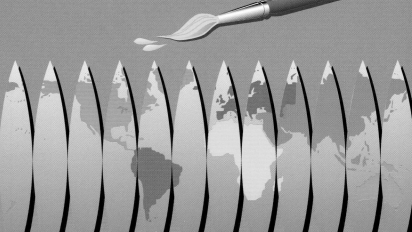

2 You could carefully peel the skin into segments.

3 Then you could lay the peel flat to make a map of the world.

4 Mapmakers fill the gaps by stretching some parts of the map and shrinking others.

On this map, you can see that more than half of the Earth is covered by four big oceans. The rest of the Earth is divided into seven huge areas of land, called continents. There are also three imaginary lines on the map. The equator circles the Earth's center. The Arctic Circle is at the top of the Earth and the Antarctic Circle is at the bottom.

ARCTIC OCEAN

Arctic Circle

NORTH AMERICA

EUROPE

ASIA

PACIFIC OCEAN

ATLANTIC OCEAN

AFRICA

Equator

SOUTH AMERICA

INDIAN OCEAN

AUSTRALIA

Antarctic Circle

ANTARCTICA

1 This is a picture of a house on the corner of Park Street, which runs through a seaside town. You can see the hedge around the house, the tree outside and some of the street, but you cannot see the town or the sea because the picture is not big enough to show all these details.

2 This map shows Park Street from above. It shows less detail but a bigger area than before. Can you spot the house on the corner? Here, Park Street measures 4 inches (10cm), but it is really 1 mile (1km) long. This means that on the map every 4 inches (10cm) is the same as 1 mile (1km) in the real place. This is called *scale*.

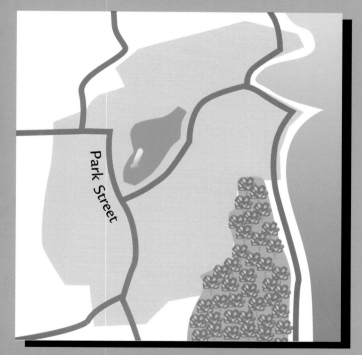

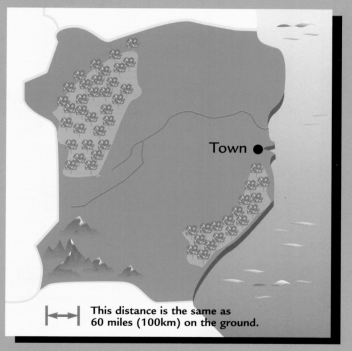

This distance is the same as 60 miles (100km) on the ground.

3 This map shows a bigger area than the last map because it has a smaller scale. It shows all of the town. You cannot see the houses or all the streets, but you can see Park Street. On this map, Park Street is 2 inches (5cm) long. This means every 2 inches (5cm) on the map is the same as 1 mile (1km) in the real place.

4 This map shows the country where the town is found. The town is shown as a dot. The scale bar tells you that $3/8$ inch (1cm) on the map is the same as 60 miles (100km) in the real place. In this atlas, each map has a different scale and scale bar. On pages 10-11 you can see all the whole world at the same scale.

Hot and cold

Around the world, there are different patterns of weather called climates. The climate of a country depends on where it is in the world. It is always hot near the equator and cold near the North and South Poles. On each map in this atlas, you will find a locator globe, showing you where countries and continents are in the world. The globe has arrows pointing to the four directions—north, south, east and west.

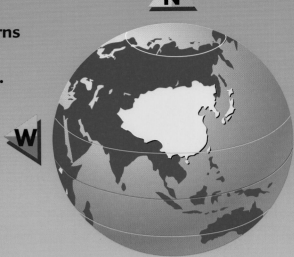

The sun warms all the countries in the world, but shines more strongly on some than others. These countries have the warmest weather. Around the world, the weather also changes at different times of year.

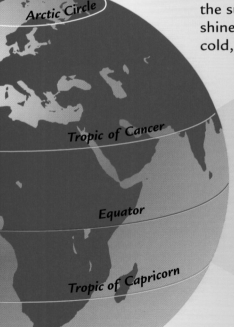

Around the North and South Poles, the sun is never high in the sky and shines weakly, so the land is always cold, especially in winter.

Near the equator, the sun shines strongest and directly from above. Here the climate is hot, with wet and dry seasons.

Above and below the equator, there are two imaginary lines called the Tropic of Cancer and the Tropic of Capricorn. Countries between the tropics and the North and South Poles have warm summers and cold winters.

Different climates suit particular kinds of plants, and make different types of land for animals and people to live in. If a place has a rainy climate, lots of plants grow. If the climate is dry, fewer and different plants grow.

On the map below and the maps in this atlas, different types of land are shown by small pictures, called symbols, and colors. These photographs show you what the land really looks like.

Usually, the poles are icy cold. In summer, a few small plants grow around the Arctic.

Deciduous forests grow in cool areas. The trees lose their leaves in autumn.

Evergreen trees stay green all year. Evergreen forests grow in cold places.

Grassland includes tropical savanna (seen here), farmland and flat plains, called pampas.

Only the toughest plants and animals are able to survive in dry deserts.

Thick, green rainforests grow where it is warm and wet all year.

Few plants grow on rocky mountains, which are often covered in snow.

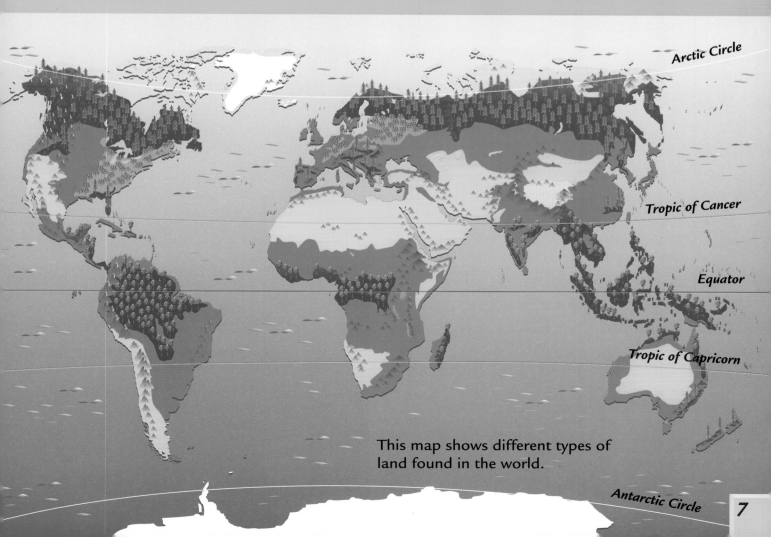

Arctic Circle

Tropic of Cancer

Equator

Tropic of Capricorn

This map shows different types of land found in the world.

Antarctic Circle

About this atlas

The maps in this atlas can tell you an enormous amount about the places they show. Look carefully at the pictures to find out more.

Each country is run from a capital city. These are shown by the flag of the country and a star.

A gray line shows a country border. When countries are arguing about a border or are not sure where the border is, the line is dotted.

A blue line shows a river. The name of the river is written alongside. Rivers can run through many countries.

Crops grow all over the world. Look out for wheat, rice, fruit and vegetables. You may see coffee, tea and sugar cane, too.

Some buildings are shown on the maps. You may see a famous monument, an old ruin or a type of home.

This picture shows where people drill into the land and seabed for oil, which is used to power all kinds of machines.

Different kinds of animals live in different parts of the world. Look for animals that live in the sea, on land and in the air.

This picture shows where people mine for diamonds. People also mine coal, silver, jewels, gold, copper, tin and iron.

Different people live around the world. Look for people playing sports or enjoying a traditional dance.

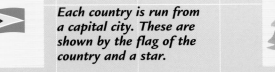

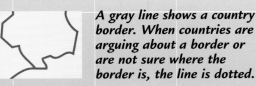
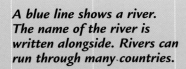

Royal gramma fish

Oil

VENEZUELA

Rice

Rice

Georgetown
GUYANA

Paramaribo
SURINAME

Cayenne
FRENCH GUIANA (France)

Diamonds

Gold

Angel Falls

Gold

Equator

Crocodile

Emerald tree boa

Piranha fish

Dug-out canoes

Amazon River

Gold

Tobacco

Sugar cane

Cotton

Cargo ships

BRAZIL

Recife

Oil

Toucan

Diamonds

Gold

Umbrella bird

Sloth

Stilt house

Rainforest clearing

São Francisco River

Oil

Shrimp

Jaguar

Vampire bat

Gold

Corn

Iron

Brasília

Cotton

Tourism

Lobster

Sugar cane

BOLIVIA

Oil

Gold

Rice

Oranges

Cotton

La Paz

Wheat

Iron

ANDES MOUNTAINS

Potatoes

Gas

Cattle ranching

Cotton

Carnival

8

E   F   G   H   I   J   K   L   M

About the Factfile

Each map has a Factfile with facts about the places you can see. You might find out about a special animal or plant from a particular part of the world. Look at the picture beside each fact and then find it on the map. The facts in this Factfile are about the map of part of South America shown on the opposite page. Can you find all the pictures on the map?

On page 42, you will find a section of fascinating facts, full of many interesting things about the countries of the world.

Factfile

South America is home to nearly one quarter of all known animals and around 2,500 different kinds of trees.

The longest mountain range in the world is the Andes in South America.

Half of all the people in South America live in Brazil.

 FACT FINDER

Each map has a grid, which divides it into squares. The columns run up and down and have letters. The rows run from side to side and have numbers. This means each square has a name, or grid reference.

The Fact Finder asks questions about places on the map. You can find the answers by looking at the grid reference.

Here is a Fact Finder question about the map of part of South America shown on the opposite page.

▶ What is the name of the highest waterfall in the world? (See square E 4.)

To find square E 4, lay your ruler on column E, at the bottom of the map. Leave the ruler lying on the map. Now put your finger on row 4, at the side of the map. Run your finger along row 4 in a straight line. Square E 4 is where your finger meets the ruler.

You should have found Angel Falls which is in Venezuela.

▼ This girl is answering the Fact Finder question. She is using a ruler and her finger to find the correct grid reference.

World map

These countries in Europe are shown more clearly inside the circle on page 11.

ARCTIC OCEAN

GREENLAND (Denmark)

ALASKA (USA)

CANADA

FINLAND

NORW

ICELAND

THE NETHERLANDS

SWEDEN

ESTONIA

LATVIA

UNITED KINGDOM

REPUBLIC OF IRELAND

BELGIUM

UNITED STATES OF AMERICA

ATLANTIC OCEAN

FRANCE

ANDORRA

SPAIN

PORTUGAL

AZORES (Portugal)

MADEIRA (Portugal)

MOROCCO

BALEARIC ISLANDS (Spain)

MALTA

TUNISIA

CRE (Gre

BERMUDA (UK)

DOMINICAN REPUBLIC

PUERTO RICO (USA)

VIRGIN ISLANDS (USA & UK)

ANGUILLA (UK)

ST. KITTS & NEVIS

ANTIGUA & BARBUDA

GUADELOUPE (France)

DOMINICA

MARTINIQUE (France)

ST. LUCIA

BARBADOS

GRENADA

TRINIDAD & TOBAGO

CANARY ISLANDS (Spain)

ALGERIA

LIBYA

MEXICO

BAHAMAS

BELIZE

CUBA

JAMAICA

HONDURAS HAITI

GUATEMALA

EL SALVADOR

NICARAGUA

MONTSERRAT (UK)

ST. VINCENT & THE GRENADINES

COSTA RICA

PANAMA

VENEZUELA

GUYANA

SURINAME

FRENCH GUIANA (France)

WESTERN SAHARA

CAPE VERDE ISLANDS

MAURITANIA

MALI

NIGER

CHAD

SENEGAL

GAMBIA

GUINEA-BISSAU

GUINEA

BURKINA FASO

SIERRA LEONE

IVORY COAST

LIBERIA

TOGO

BENIN

GHANA

NIGERIA

CENTR AFRIC REPUB

CAMEROON

SÃO TOMÉ & PRÍNCIPE

EQUATORIAL GUINEA

GABON

CONGO

DEMOC REPU OF CO

GALAPAGOS ISLANDS (Ecuador)

ECUADOR

COLOMBIA

PERU

BRAZIL

PACIFIC OCEAN

CABINDA (Angola)

ANGOLA

ZAM

NAMIBIA

BOLIVIA

PARAGUAY

BOTSWANA

ATLANTIC OCEAN

REPUBLIC O SOUTH AFRIC

CHILE

URUGUAY

ARGENTINA

LESOTH

FALKLAND ISLANDS (UK)

SOUTH GEORGIA (UK)

The world is divided into almost 200 countries and this map shows most of them. The countries are different colors so that you can tell them apart. Some countries own places in other parts of the world. In this atlas, these kinds of places have two labels. One label gives their name and another label in brackets gives the name of the country that owns them.

ANTARCTIC

RUSSIA

KAZAKSTAN

AZERBAIJAN

ARMENIA
RGIA
RKEY
US
SYRIA
LEBANON
IRAQ
RDAN
QATAR
SAUDI
ARABIA
OMAN

UZBEKISTAN

TURKMENISTAN

TAJIKISTAN

KYRGYZSTAN

MONGOLIA

NORTH
KOREA

JAPAN

SOUTH
KOREA

CHINA

AFGHANISTAN

IRAN

PACIFIC
OCEAN

KUWAIT

BAHRAIN

PAKISTAN

BHUTAN

NEPAL

MACAU
(Portugal)

TAIWAN
(China)

UNITED
ARAB
EMIRATES

INDIA

MYANMAR

HONG
KONG
(China)

ERITREA YEMEN

DJIBOUTI

ETHIOPIA

SOCOTRA
(Yemen)

BANGLADESH

ANDAMAN
ISLANDS
(India)

LAOS

THAILAND

VIETNAM

CAMBODIA

NORTHERN
MARIANAS
(USA)

GUAM (USA)

MARSHALL
ISLANDS

PHILIPPINES

MALDIVE
ISLANDS

NICOBAR
ISLANDS
(India)

SRI
LANKA

BRUNEI

PALAU
(USA)

NDA

SOMALIA

KENYA

RWANDA

BURUNDI

ANIA MALAWI

COMOROS

SEYCHELLES

INDIAN
OCEAN

SINGAPORE

MALAYSIA

STATES OF MICRONESIA

NAURU

KIRIBATI

I N D O N E S I A

IRIAN JAYA
(Indonesia)

PAPUA NEW
GUINEA

TUVALU

SOLOMON
ISLANDS

MAYOTTE (France)

MBABWE

MADAGASCAR

AMBIQUE

AZILAND

SWEDEN

DENMARK

LATVIA

LITHUANIA

(Russia)

BELARUS

GERMANY

POLAND

VANUATU

AUSTRALIA

FIJI

NEW
CALEDONIA
(France)

LUXEMBOURG

CZECH
REPUBLIC

SLOVAKIA

UKRAINE

LIECHTENSTEIN

AUSTRIA

HUNGARY

MOLDOVA

SWITZERLAND

SLOVENIA

ROMANIA

SAN
MARINO

CROATIA

FEDERAL
REPUBLIC OF
YUGOSLAVIA

MONACO

BOSNIA-
HERZEGOVINA

CORSICA
(France)

ITALY

BULGARIA

TASMANIA
(Australia)

NEW ZEALAND

MACEDONIA

SARDINIA
(Italy)

VATICAN
CITY

ALBANIA

TURKEY

SICILY
(Italy)

GREECE

Some countries in Europe are
crowded together. In this circle,
we have made these countries
bigger so that you can see
them more easily.

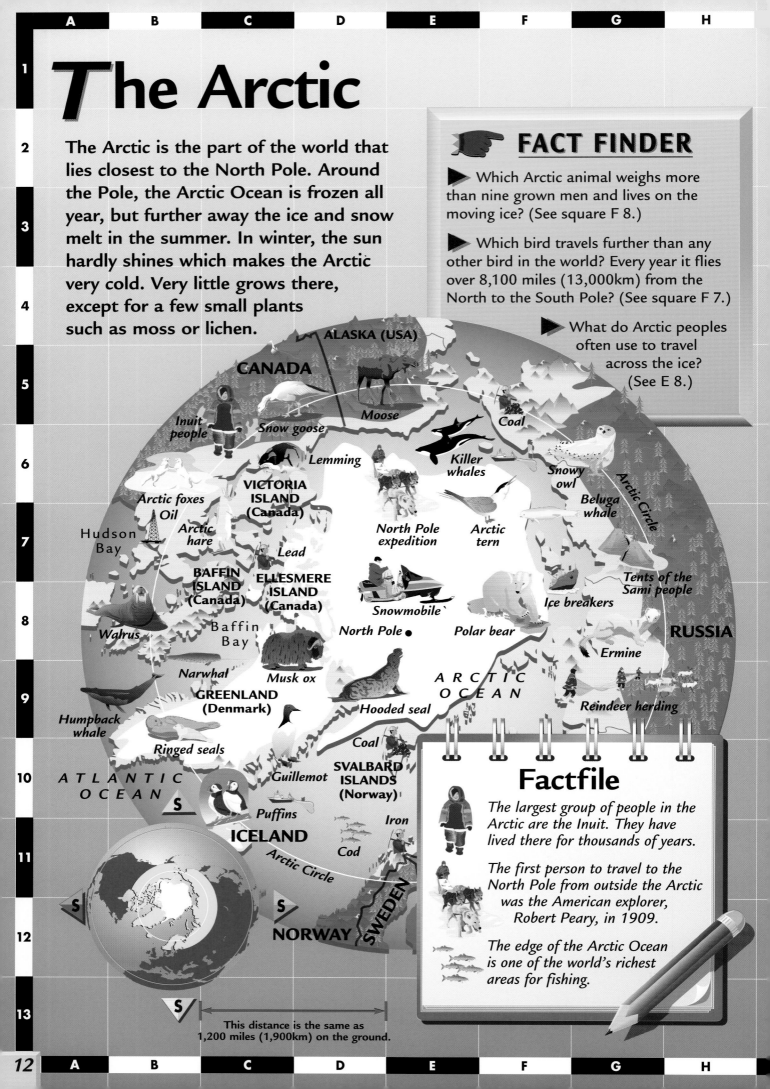

The Arctic

The Arctic is the part of the world that lies closest to the North Pole. Around the Pole, the Arctic Ocean is frozen all year, but further away the ice and snow melt in the summer. In winter, the sun hardly shines which makes the Arctic very cold. Very little grows there, except for a few small plants such as moss or lichen.

FACT FINDER

▶ Which Arctic animal weighs more than nine grown men and lives on the moving ice? (See square F 8.)

▶ Which bird travels further than any other bird in the world? Every year it flies over 8,100 miles (13,000km) from the North to the South Pole? (See square F 7.)

▶ What do Arctic peoples often use to travel across the ice? (See E 8.)

ALASKA (USA)

CANADA

Inuit people

Snow goose

Moose

Coal

Killer whales

Lemming

Snowy owl

Arctic foxes

Oil

VICTORIA ISLAND (Canada)

Arctic Circle

Beluga whale

Hudson Bay

Arctic hare

North Pole expedition

Arctic tern

Lead

BAFFIN ISLAND (Canada)

ELLESMERE ISLAND (Canada)

Tents of the Sami people

Ice breakers

Walrus

Baffin Bay

Snowmobile

North Pole ●

Polar bear

RUSSIA

Ermine

Narwhal

Musk ox

A R C T I C   O C E A N

GREENLAND (Denmark)

Hooded seal

Reindeer herding

Humpback whale

Ringed seals

Coal

A T L A N T I C   O C E A N

Guillemot

SVALBARD ISLANDS (Norway)

S

Puffins

Iron

ICELAND

Cod

Arctic Circle

S

S

NORWAY

SWEDEN

S

This distance is the same as 1,200 miles (1,900km) on the ground.

Factfile

The largest group of people in the Arctic are the Inuit. They have lived there for thousands of years.

The first person to travel to the North Pole from outside the Arctic was the American explorer, Robert Peary, in 1909.

The edge of the Arctic Ocean is one of the world's richest areas for fishing.

Antarctica

Antarctica is an enormous ice-covered continent near the South Pole. It is the coldest and windiest place on Earth. Few animals live around the pole but there are seals and birds on the coast, and plants and fish in the sea. The only people living in Antarctica are scientists. They stay on research stations to study the land and its wildlife.

Factfile

In 1911, Roald Amundsen, a Norwegian explorer, became the first person to reach the South Pole.

Up to 30,000 tourists a year cruise the waters around Antarctica to see the land and its wildlife.

Antarctica has many icebergs. The largest one ever found was three times the size of the island of Cyprus.

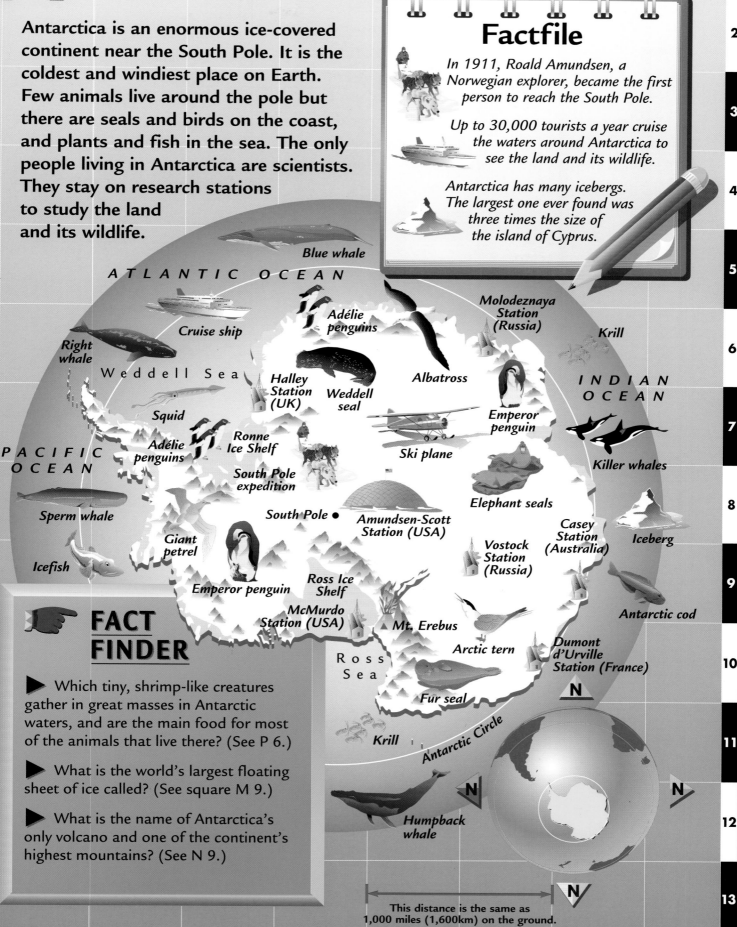

Blue whale

ATLANTIC OCEAN

Cruise ship

Adélie penguins

Molodeznaya Station (Russia)

Krill

Right whale

Weddell Sea

Halley Station (UK)

Weddell seal

Albatross

INDIAN OCEAN

Squid

Ronne Ice Shelf

Ski plane

Emperor penguin

Adélie penguins

PACIFIC OCEAN

South Pole expedition

Killer whales

Elephant seals

Sperm whale

South Pole ●

Amundsen-Scott Station (USA)

Casey Station (Australia)

Iceberg

Giant petrel

Vostock Station (Russia)

Icefish

Emperor penguin

Ross Ice Shelf

Antarctic cod

McMurdo Station (USA)

Mt. Erebus

Dumont d'Urville Station (France)

Arctic tern

Ross Sea

N

Fur seal

Krill

Antarctic Circle

Humpback whale

N

N

N

This distance is the same as 1,000 miles (1,600km) on the ground.

FACT FINDER

▶ Which tiny, shrimp-like creatures gather in great masses in Antarctic waters, and are the main food for most of the animals that live there? (See P 6.)

▶ What is the world's largest floating sheet of ice called? (See square M 9.)

▶ What is the name of Antarctica's only volcano and one of the continent's highest mountains? (See N 9.)

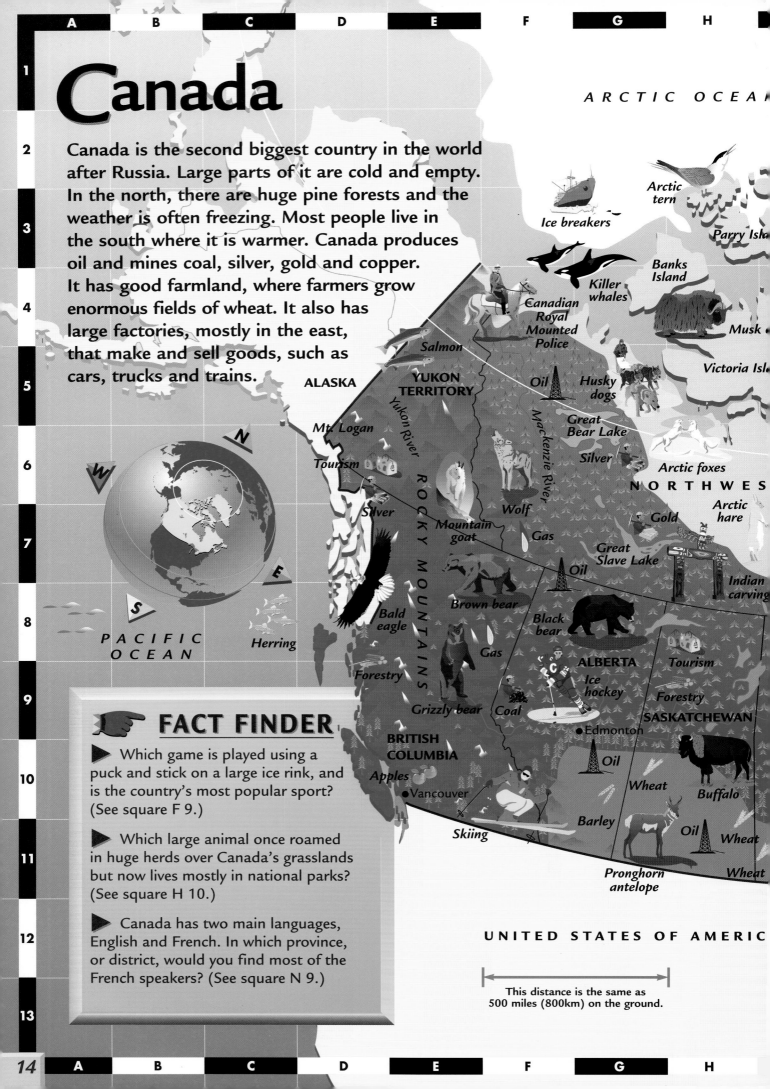

Canada

Canada is the second biggest country in the world after Russia. Large parts of it are cold and empty. In the north, there are huge pine forests and the weather is often freezing. Most people live in the south where it is warmer. Canada produces oil and mines coal, silver, gold and copper. It has good farmland, where farmers grow enormous fields of wheat. It also has large factories, mostly in the east, that make and sell goods, such as cars, trucks and trains.

FACT FINDER

▶ Which game is played using a puck and stick on a large ice rink, and is the country's most popular sport? (See square F 9.)

▶ Which large animal once roamed in huge herds over Canada's grasslands but now lives mostly in national parks? (See square H 10.)

▶ Canada has two main languages, English and French. In which province, or district, would you find most of the French speakers? (See square N 9.)

This distance is the same as 500 miles (800km) on the ground.

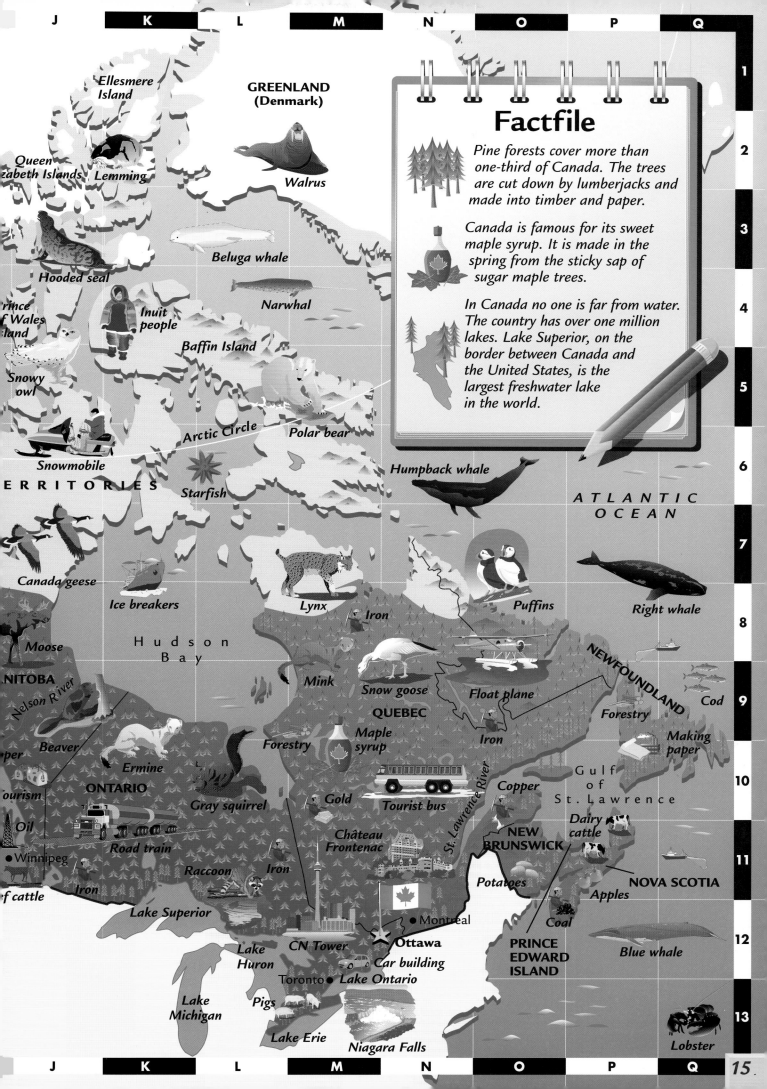

Factfile

Pine forests cover more than one-third of Canada. The trees are cut down by lumberjacks and made into timber and paper.

Canada is famous for its sweet maple syrup. It is made in the spring from the sticky sap of sugar maple trees.

In Canada no one is far from water. The country has over one million lakes. Lake Superior, on the border between Canada and the United States, is the largest freshwater lake in the world.

Ellesmere Island

GREENLAND (Denmark)

Queen Elizabeth Islands

Lemming

Walrus

Hooded seal

Beluga whale

Narwhal

Inuit people

Prince of Wales Island

Baffin Island

Snowy owl

Snowmobile

Arctic Circle

Polar bear

Humpback whale

ATLANTIC OCEAN

TERRITORIES

Starfish

Canada geese

Ice breakers

Lynx

Iron

Puffins

Right whale

Moose

Hudson Bay

Mink

Snow goose

Float plane

NEWFOUNDLAND

Cod

MANITOBA

Nelson River

Forestry

QUEBEC

Iron

Forestry

Making paper

Copper

Beaver

Ermine

Maple syrup

Gulf of St. Lawrence

Ontario

Gray squirrel

Gold

Tourist bus

Copper

Dairy cattle

Tourism

Oil

Road train

Raccoon

Iron

Château Frontenac

NEW BRUNSWICK

Potatoes

NOVA SCOTIA

Apples

Winnipeg

Lake Superior

CN Tower

Montreal

Coal

Beef cattle

Iron

Lake Huron

Toronto

Ottawa

Car building

Lake Ontario

PRINCE EDWARD ISLAND

Blue whale

Lake Michigan

Pigs

Lake Erie

Niagara Falls

Lobster

J K L M N O P Q

1 2 3 4 5 6 7 8 9 10 11 12 13

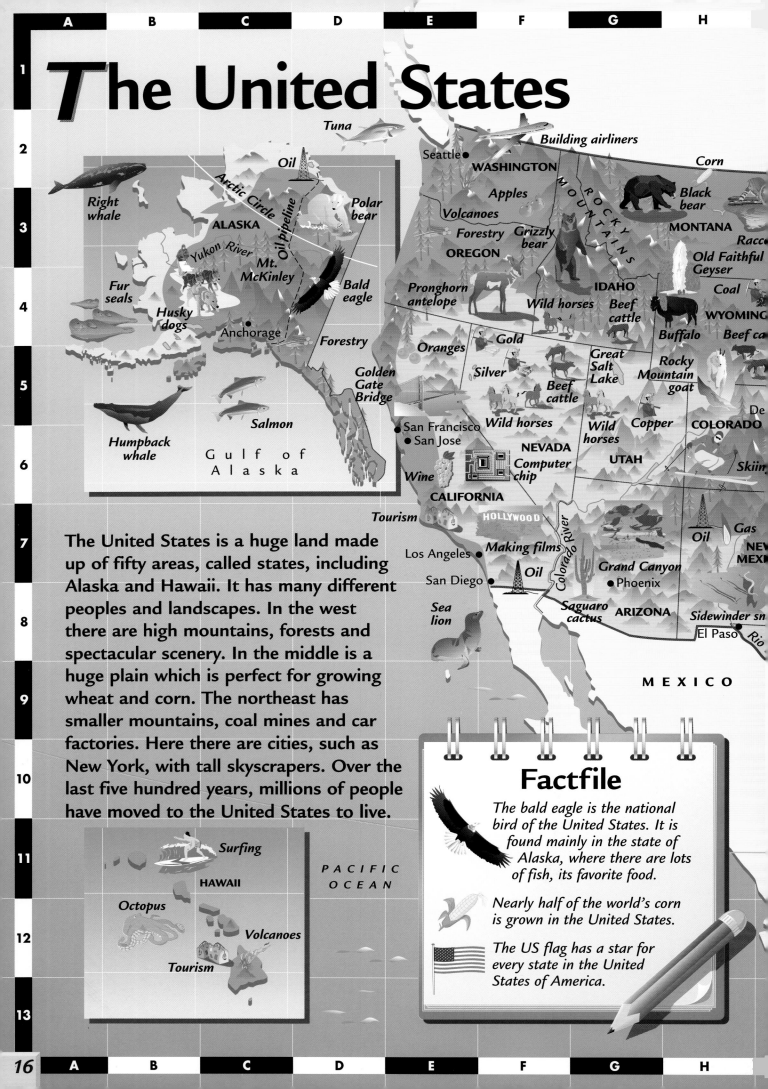

The United States

The United States is a huge land made up of fifty areas, called states, including Alaska and Hawaii. It has many different peoples and landscapes. In the west there are high mountains, forests and spectacular scenery. In the middle is a huge plain which is perfect for growing wheat and corn. The northeast has smaller mountains, coal mines and car factories. Here there are cities, such as New York, with tall skyscrapers. Over the last five hundred years, millions of people have moved to the United States to live.

Factfile

The bald eagle is the national bird of the United States. It is found mainly in the state of Alaska, where there are lots of fish, its favorite food.

Nearly half of the world's corn is grown in the United States.

The US flag has a star for every state in the United States of America.

Map labels:

Tuna · Building airliners · Corn · Seattle · WASHINGTON · Apples · Black bear · Oil · Arctic Circle · Volcanoes · Forestry · Grizzly bear · MONTANA · Racco · Right whale · ALASKA · Polar bear · Oil pipeline · OREGON · Old Faithful Geyser · Yukon River · Mt. McKinley · Bald eagle · Pronghorn antelope · Wild horses · IDAHO · Coal · Fur seals · Beef cattle · WYOMING · Husky dogs · Anchorage · Forestry · Oranges · Gold · Great Salt Lake · Buffalo · Beef ca · Silver · Rocky Mountain goat · Golden Gate Bridge · Beef cattle · Copper · COLORADO · De · Salmon · San Francisco · San Jose · Wild horses · Wild horses · UTAH · Skiin · Humpback whale · Gulf of Alaska · NEVADA · Computer chip · Wine · CALIFORNIA · HOLLYWOOD · Colorado River · Oil · Gas · NEW MEXI · Tourism · Making films · Grand Canyon · Los Angeles · Oil · Phoenix · San Diego · Saguaro cactus · ARIZONA · Sidewinder sn · Sea lion · El Paso · Rio · MEXICO · Surfing · PACIFIC OCEAN · HAWAII · Octopus · Volcanoes · Tourism · ROCKY MOUNTAINS

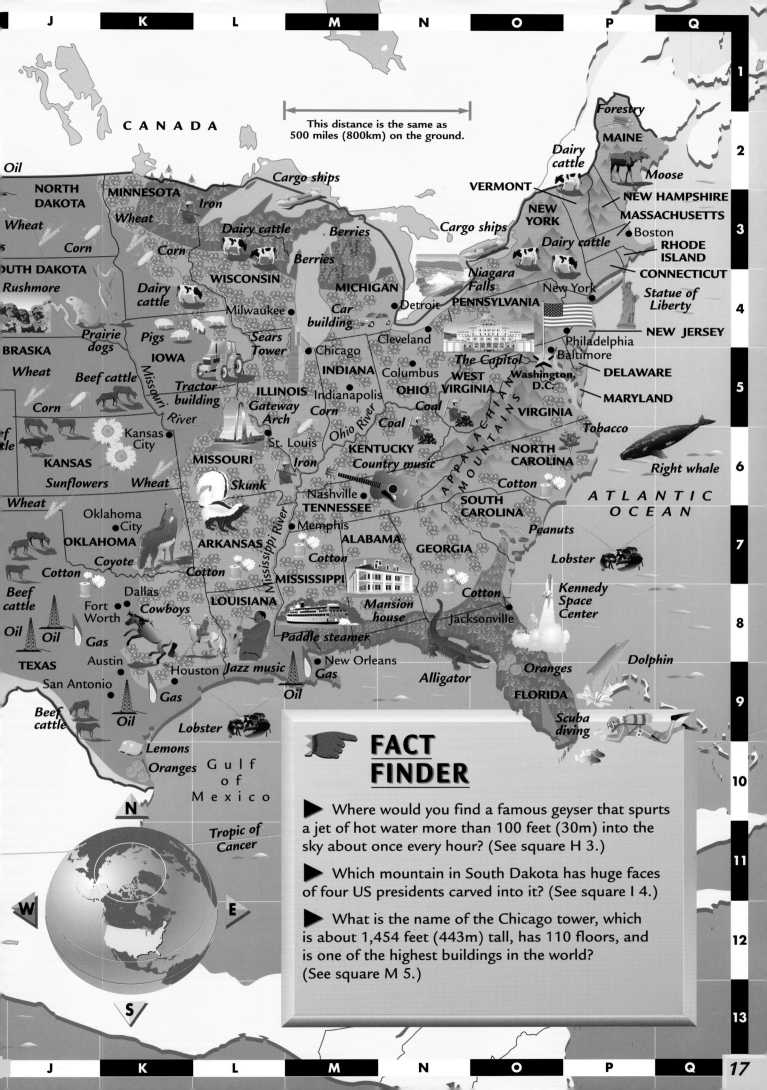

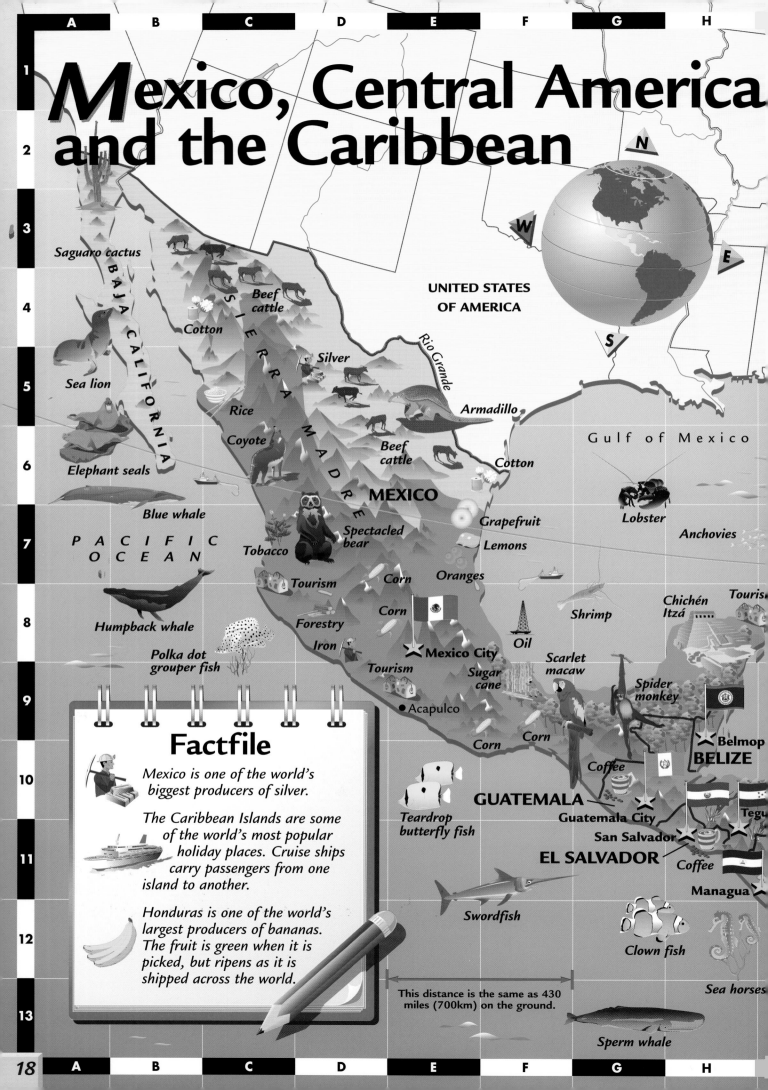

Mexico, Central America and the Caribbean

A B C D E F G H

1 2 3 4 5 6 7 8 9 10 11 12 13

N
W E
S

Saguaro cactus

BAJA CALIFORNIA

SIERRA MADRE

Beef cattle

Cotton

Silver

Sea lion

Rice

Coyote

Elephant seals

Blue whale

P A C I F I C
O C E A N

Humpback whale

Polka dot grouper fish

Tobacco

Tourism

Forestry

Iron

Spectacled bear

Corn

Corn

Tourism

Mexico City

Acapulco

Corn

Corn

MEXICO

Armadillo

Cotton

Grapefruit

Lemons

Oranges

Rio Grande

UNITED STATES OF AMERICA

Gulf of Mexico

Lobster

Anchovies

Shrimp

Oil

Sugar cane

Scarlet macaw

Spider monkey

Chichén Itzá

Touris

Belmop

BELIZE

Coffee

GUATEMALA

Guatemala City

San Salvador

EL SALVADOR

Coffee

Tegu

Managua

Teardrop butterfly fish

Swordfish

Clown fish

Sea horses

Sperm whale

This distance is the same as 430 miles (700km) on the ground.

Factfile

Mexico is one of the world's biggest producers of silver.

The Caribbean Islands are some of the world's most popular holiday places. Cruise ships carry passengers from one island to another.

Honduras is one of the world's largest producers of bananas. The fruit is green when it is picked, but ripens as it is shipped across the world.

18

A B C D E F G H

To the south of the United States, a narrow strip of land containing eight countries links North America with South America. The largest of these is Mexico, a country with a long history and contrasting landscapes. Further south are the seven nations of Central America. Many people in Central America are farmers, who grow food for themselves or work on sugar, coffee or banana plantations. Further east, in the warm Caribbean Sea, lie hundreds of sun-drenched islands. They are famous for their coral reefs and beautiful sandy beaches.

FACT FINDER

▶ In Central America, which ancient city was built by an American Indian people called the Maya over one thousand years ago? (See square H 8.)

▶ Which shortcut is used by cargo ships to sail between the Atlantic and Pacific Oceans. It is about 51 miles (82km) long and about 30 ships pass through it each day. (See square K 12.)

▶ Which is the only kind of bear to live in Central America? It is named after the white circles around its eyes. (See D 7.)

▶ Which is one of the largest cities in the world, where more people live than in the whole of Australia? (See square E 8.)

Tourism

Reef sharks

ATLANTIC OCEAN

BAHAMAS

Tropic of Cancer

Cruise ship

Havana

Beef cattle

CUBA

Tourism

DOMINICAN REPUBLIC

Hummingbird

VIRGIN ISLANDS (USA & UK)

ANGUILLA

Flamingoes

Tobacco

Coffee

HAITI

San Juan

ANTIGUA & BARBUDA

GUADELOUPE (France)

G R E A T E R

Port-au-Prince

Santo Domingo

PUERTO RICO (USA)

ST. KITTS & NEVIS

Tuna

Tourism

A N T I L L E S

LESSER ANTILLES

DOMINICA

Tourism

MARTINIQUE (France)

JAMAICA

Kingston

ST. LUCIA

BARBADOS

ONDURAS

Dolphin

Sailing

ST. VINCENT & THE GRENADINES

Bananas

C a r i b b e a n   S e a

GRENADA

Anole lizard

Royal gramma fish

Scuba diving

TRINIDAD & TOBAGO

ARAGUA

CURAÇAO (Netherlands)

Oil

Cotton

Leatherback turtle

Panama Canal

Toucan

Cargo ships

San José

Panama City

ee

PANAMA

VENEZUELA

OSTA ICA

COLOMBIA

Cargo ship in Panama Canal

South America

The continent of South America stretches from the warm Caribbean Sea to the stormy waters around Cape Horn. South America is warm all year, except in the far south and in the high Andes Mountains. In the north, the great Amazon River flows through tropical rain forest. Farther south, there are flat plains where millions of cattle graze. Most South Americans live in cities on the coast. In the country, the farmers grow bananas, coffee beans, and corn.

Caribbean Sea

Cargo ships

Royal gramma fish

Tourism
Bananas
Gold
Emeralds

Oil
Oil

Oil
Coffee
Bogotá
Coffee
Herring
Bananas
Coffee
Oil
Cali
Quito
ECUADOR
COLOMBIA
Bananas
Oil
Cotton
Oil

VENEZUELA
Caracas
Oil
Orinoco River
Cow tree
Diamonds
Making clothes
Gold
Stilt house
Tapir
Copper
Llama
Sugar cane
Lima
PERU
Gold
Lake Titicaca
Arrow-poison frog
Umbrella bird

Rice
Georgetown
GUYANA
Angel Falls
Gold

Rice
Paramaribo
SURINAME
Gold

Cayenne
FRENCH GUIANA (France)

Equator
Shrimp
Crocodile
Emerald tree boa
Piranha fish
Oil
Dug-out canoes
Amazon River
Sloth
Jaguar
Gold
Sugar cane
Potatoes
Cotton
BOLIVIA
La Paz
Gas
Oil
Gold
Corn Cotton
Cattle ranching
Wheat
Rice
Oranges
Iron
Tourism

Amazon rain forest
Vampire bat
Toucan
Corn
Iron
Rain forest clearing
Diamonds
Gold
BRAZIL
Brasília
São Francisco River
Cotton

Tobacco
Cotton
Gold
Oil
Sugar cane
Cotton
Recife
Cargo ships
Shrimp
Lobster
Carnival

Sperm whale

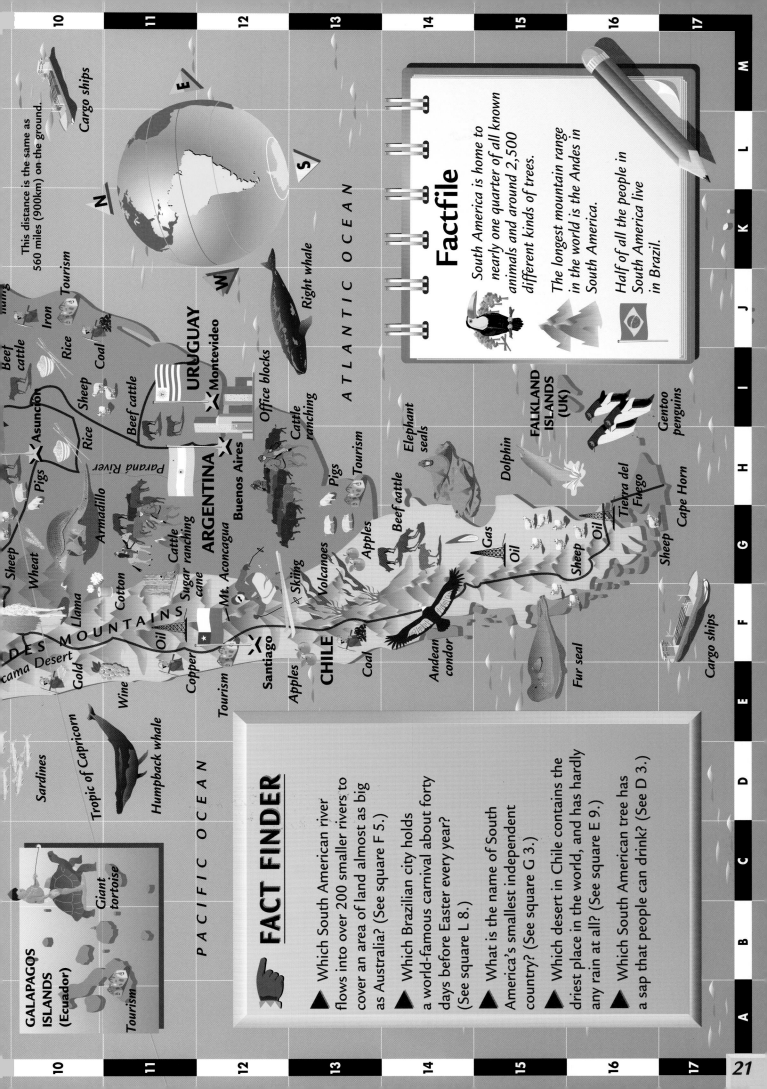

This distance is the same as 560 miles (900km) on the ground.

N
E
S
W

Cargo ships

ATLANTIC OCEAN

Right whale

URUGUAY
Montevideo

Beef cattle
Iron
Tourism
Rice
Coal
Sheep
Rice
Beef cattle

Office blocks

Cattle ranching

ARGENTINA
Buenos Aires

Pigs
Tourism

Elephant seals

Apples

Beef cattle

Dolphin

Gas
Oil

FALKLAND ISLANDS
(UK)

Sheep
Oil

Tierra del Fuego

Gentoo penguins

Cape Horn

Sheep

Fur seal

Volcanoes
Skiing

Andean condor

Coal

CHILE
Santiago

Apples
Tourism

Copper
Oil

Wine
Gold

Cotton
Llama

Sheep
Wheat

ANDES MOUNTAINS
Atacama Desert

Mt. Aconcagua
Sugar cane
Cattle ranching

Parana River

Asuncion
Pigs
Armadillo

Cargo ships

Factfile

South America is home to nearly one quarter of all known animals and around 2,500 different kinds of trees.

The longest mountain range in the world is the Andes in South America.

Half of all the people in South America live in Brazil.

PACIFIC OCEAN

Sardines
Tropic of Capricorn
Humpback whale

GALAPAGOS ISLANDS
(Ecuador)

Giant tortoise

Tourism

FACT FINDER

▲ Which South American river flows into over 200 smaller rivers to cover an area of land almost as big as Australia? (See square F 5.)

▲ Which Brazilian city holds a world-famous carnival about forty days before Easter every year? (See square L 8.)

▲ What is the name of South America's smallest independent country? (See square G 3.)

▲ Which desert in Chile contains the driest place in the world, and has hardly any rain at all? (See square E 9.)

▲ Which South American tree has a sap that people can drink? (See D 3.)

Northern Europe

Narwhal

Arctic Circ

Northern Europe is a cool part of the world where it can rain at any time of year. It has mountains and pine forests in the far north, and higher mountains in the south. In between lies flat land that was once covered by forest. Over hundreds of years, the trees have been cleared to make room for farms, towns, and cities. Most northern Europeans live in towns and work in factories, shops and offices.

Arctic Circle

Puffins

ICELAND

Strokkur geyser

Reykjavík

Sheep

Arctic tern

Viking longship remains

Trondh

Skiing
Mt. Glitterting

Gas

Oil

Shetland pony

Bergen

Making paper

Oslo

Oil Gas

Herring

NORWAY

Cod

Osprey

ATLANTIC OCEAN

Cod

Ship building

North Sea

NORTHERN IRELAND (UK)

Red deer

Edinburgh

Dairy cattle

Salmon

Belfast

Car building

Gas

Oil

Pigs

REPUBLIC OF IRELAND

Stoat

UNITED KINGDOM

Thresher shark

DENMARK

Copenhage

Dublin

THE NETHERLANDS

Pigs

Ship build

Dairy cattle

Potatoes

Clogs

Harbor porpoise

Sheep

Badger

Dairy cattle

Elbe River

Ott

Starfish

Cardiff

London

Amsterdam

Windmills

Hedgehog

Wild ponies

Stonehenge

BELGIUM

GERMANY

Lobster

Channel Tunnel

Brussels

Car buildi

Tourism

LUXEMBOURG

Coal

Chotolate

Paris

Frankfurt

Cheese

Eiffel Tower

Luxembourg

Wine

Forestry

This distance is the same as 300 miles (480km) on the ground.

Loire River

Seine River

Rhine River

Neuschwanstein castle

Wine

Gray heron

Woodpecker

Wine

FRANCE

LIECHTENSTE

B a y o f B i s c a y

Wine

High-speed trains

Bern

ALPS

Watches

Bordeaux

Rhône River

SWITZERLAND

Ski

Norwegian
Sea

KJØLEN MOUNTAINS

Lapland

Reindeer

Sami people

Iron

Forestry

Cross-country skiing

Forestry

Lynx

Making
paper

SWEDEN

FINLAND

Making paper

Salmon

Helsinki

Herring

Fox

Tallinn

Stockholm

Ice
breakers

Pigs

ESTONIA

building

Dairy
cattle

Building
trains

eborg

Riga

LATVIA

B a l t i c
S e a

LITHUANIA

Malmö

Vilnius

Ship building

Kaliningrad
(Russia)

BELARUS

p building

Dairy cattle

Potatoes

Red squirrel

Chaffinch

Warsaw

Wild boar

POLAND

Coal

Wolf

UKRAINE

lir

Prague
**CZECH
REPUBLIC**

Chamois

SLOVAKIA

Vienna

USTRIA

Bratislava

River

Peregrine
falcon

Budapest

Parliament
building

ROMANIA

HUNGARY

Wild horses

FACT FINDER

► Which tunnel in northern Europe is about 31 miles (50km) long and allows 400 trains to pass along it in each direction every day? (See square E 10.)

► In which country could you see a long ship on display, which was built by the Viking people hundreds of years ago? (See square H 4.)

► Which famous European tower is about 984 feet (320m) high and has 1,652 steps that take you to the top? (See square E 11.)

► Which stone monument in England was built around 3,500 years ago, but nobody knows what it was used for? (See square E 10.)

RUSSIA

N

W   E

S

Factfile

There are twice as many pigs in Denmark as people. Two out of three pigs are exported as Danish bacon.

France is visited by more tourists each year than any other country in the world.

Finland produces enough paper to make 5 million comics every day.

Southern Europe

ATLANTIC OCEAN

Cod

Starfish

Anchovies

Thresher shark

Lobster

Harbor porpoise

Tourism

Cheese

Wine

Eiffel Tower

Paris
Seine River

BELGIUM

LUXEMBOUR

Car building

Champagne

Potatoes

Loire River

Gray heron

FRANCE

Pigs

High-speed tra

Dairy cattle

SWITZERLA

Beef cattle

Lyon

Wine

Sheep

Roe deer

Mi

A L P S

Turin

Car building
Ger

Beef cattle

Iron

Potatoes

Wolf

Wild horses

Porto

Bullfighter

Peregrine falcon

Skiing

Building airliners

Flamingoes

Ship building

Tourism

MONAC

Wheat

PYRENEES

ANDORRA

Marseille

Sagrada Familia Cathedral

Cargo ships

Olives

PORTUGAL

Sheep

Car building

Madrid

Sheep

Wheat

Barcelona

CORSICA
(France)

She

Oranges

Anchovies

Lisbon Windmill

Tagus River

Lemons

Iron

SPAIN

Olives

Sunflowers

Sailing

Squid

Golden eagle

Sheep

MAJORCA
(Spain)

MINORCA
(Spain)

SARDINIA
(Italy)

She

Wine

Avocet

Wine

Lynx

Seville

IBIZA
(Spain)

Tourism

Lobster

Tourism

Scuba diving

Flamenco dancers

Skiing

Tourism

GIBRALTAR (UK)

Anchovies

M e d i t e r r a n e a n   S e a

Southern Europe is warm, sunny and mainly dry. Large parts of it are covered with mountains and hills, but there is still plenty of good farmland. Many people in southern Europe are farmers. They grow cereals and all kinds of fruit and vegetables. Southern Europe also has many famous ancient buildings and works of art. Each year millions of tourists visit its museums and art galleries.

FACT FINDER

▶ Which Italian bell tower, built over 300 years ago, began to lean before it was even finished? (See square I 6.)

▶ What is the name of the ancient Roman stadium where gladiators once fought with swords and nets? (See J 7.)

▶ Which ancient Greek temple was built to worship the goddess Athene, protector of Athens? (See square N 8.)

Factfile

Mount Etna in Sicily is the largest volcano in Europe. It last erupted in 1995.

Spain produces more olive oil than any other country. Each year it produces enough olive oil to fill 160 Olympic-sized swimming pools.

This distance is the same as 250 miles (400km) on the ground.

Russia and its neighbors

A B C D E F G H

ARCTIC OCEAN

EUROPE

Arctic Circle

SWEDEN

FINLAND

Murmansk

Ice breakers

Reindeer

Ice break...

Kaliningrad (Russia)

St. Petersburg

Russian dolls

Archangel

Forestry

Snowy owl

Winter of Nen... peopl...

Badger

Forestry

Potatoes

Coal

Gas

Minsk

BELARUS

Bolshoi Ballet

Gas

Chisinau

Sugar beet

Kiev

Moscow

Nizhniy Novgorod

Oil

Wol...

MOLDOVA

UKRAINE

Potatoes

St. Basil's Cathedral

Car building

Ob River

URAL MOUNTAINS

Tourism

Corn

Coal

Don River

Sugar beet

Tractor building

Barley

R U ... S

Black Sea

Wine

Volga River

Oil

Gold

Hamster

Volgograd

Iron

Wheat

TURKEY

Wheat

Pigs

Crane

S t e p p e

GEORGIA

Mt. Elbrus

Pelican

Baikonur Space Center

Beef cattle

Tbilisi

Sturgeon

KAZAKSTAN

Irtysh River

ARMENIA

Yerevan

Oil

Iron

Copper

Gymnastics

Sunflowe...

AZERBAIJAN

Cotton

Baku

Caspian Sea

Aral Sea

Cotton

Tobacco

Kara Kum Desert

UZBEKISTAN

Bishkek

Almaty

Gas

Gas

Cotton

Tashkent

KYRGYZST...

Carpet weaving

Amu Darya River

Dushanbe

Wild horses

Ashgabat

Cotton

TURKMENISTAN

Oil

TAJIKISTAN

A S I A

FACT FINDER

▶ Which space center launched the world's first astronaut, Yuri Gagarin, into space in 1961? (See square G 8.)

▶ Which Russian railway line is the longest railway line in the world? It takes just over eight days to travel along it from one end to the other. (See J 8.)

This distance is the same as 700 miles (1,100km) on the ground.

26

Russia stretches across Europe and Asia and is the largest country in the world. Russia and its neighbors used to be called the Soviet Union, but in 1991 the Union split up. Most Russians live in the part of Russia that is in Europe, which has many cities and good farmland. Far away to the north and east is a huge forest called the taiga, where wolves and bears roam.

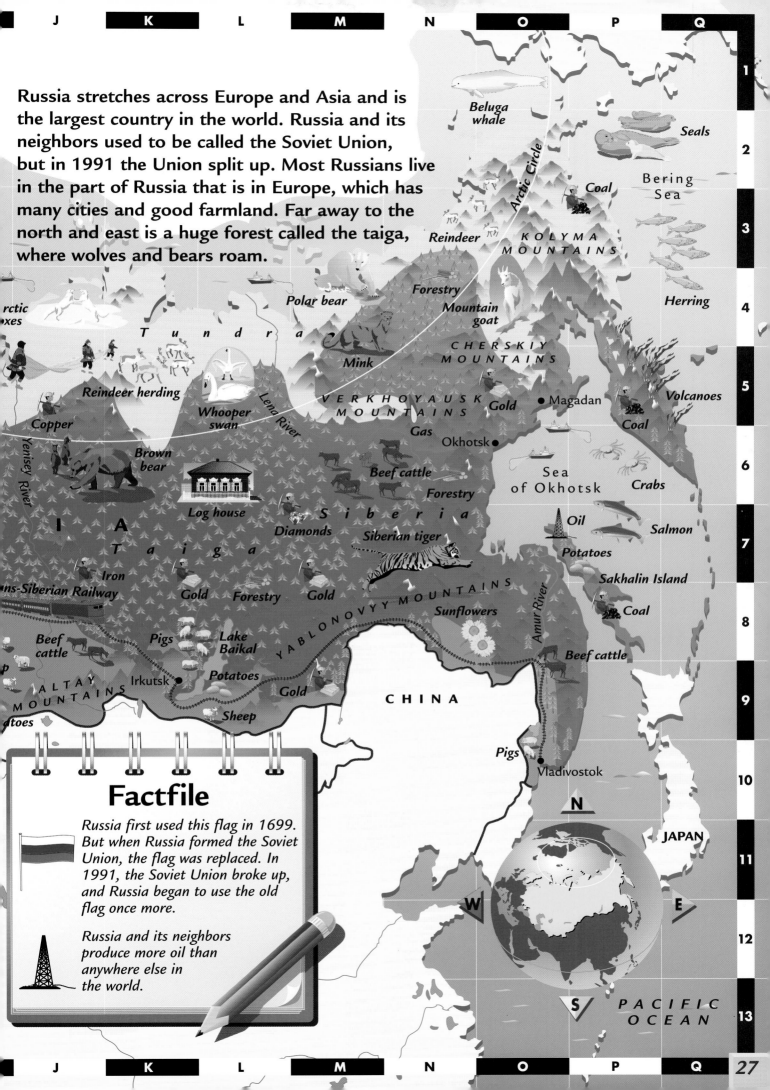

Beluga whale

Seals

Bering Sea

Arctic Circle

Coal

Herring

KOLYMA MOUNTAINS

Reindeer

Forestry

Mountain goat

Polar bear

CHERSKIY MOUNTAINS

Mink

rctic xes

Tundra

VERKHOYAUSK MOUNTAINS

Gold

Magadan

Volcanoes

Reindeer herding

Coal

Copper

Whooper swan

Lena River

Gas

Okhotsk

Brown bear

Beef cattle

Sea of Okhotsk

Crabs

Yenisey River

Log house

Forestry

Siberia

Oil

Salmon

I A

Diamonds

Siberian tiger

Potatoes

T a i g a

Sakhalin Island

Iron

ns-Siberian Railway

Gold

Forestry

Gold

YABLONOVYY MOUNTAINS

Sunflowers

Coal

Beef cattle

Amur River

Beef cattle

Pigs

Lake Baikal

Potatoes

Irkutsk

Gold

CHINA

ALTAY MOUNTAINS

Sheep

atoes

Pigs

Vladivostok

N

JAPAN

W

E

Factfile

Russia first used this flag in 1699. But when Russia formed the Soviet Union, the flag was replaced. In 1991, the Soviet Union broke up, and Russia began to use the old flag once more.

Russia and its neighbors produce more oil than anywhere else in the world.

S

PACIFIC OCEAN

The Middle East

The southwest corner of Asia is also called the Middle East. Here, thousands of years ago, people first became farmers, then settled close together in towns. Much of the land in southwest Asia is hot, dry desert, which can be hard to farm. Fifty years ago, people found oil under the desert. They used the money they made from the oil to build huge watering systems, so they could grow crops more easily in the poor soil. They also built large cities.

Factfile

Over 5,000 years ago, the first cities in the world grew up in southwest Asia, along the Tigris and Euphrates Rivers.

Three of the world's major religions began in southwest Asia. They are Islam, Judaism and Christianity.

The Middle East makes some of the world's most expensive hand-made carpets. Carpet-makers weave and knot wool to make different patterns which can tell you the area the carpet comes from.

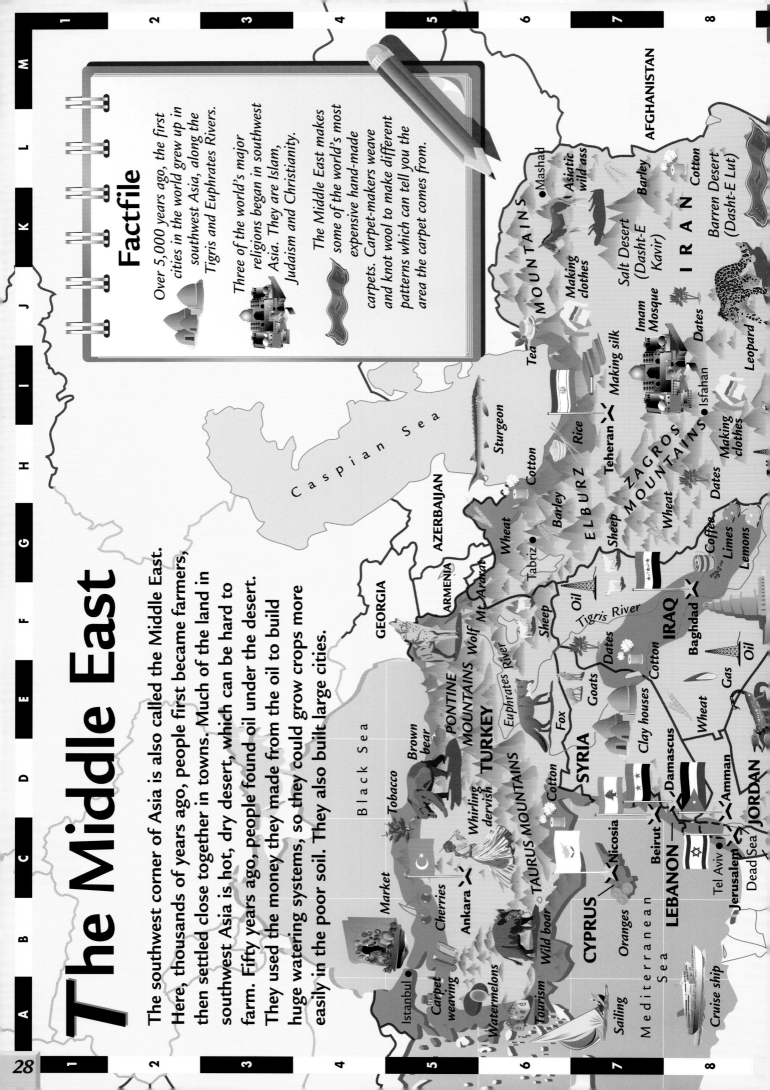

Black Sea

Caspian Sea

Mediterranean Sea

Dead Sea

GEORGIA

ARMENIA

AZERBAIJAN

TURKEY

CYPRUS

SYRIA

LEBANON

JORDAN

IRAQ

IRAN

AFGHANISTAN

PONTINE MOUNTAINS

TAURUS MOUNTAINS

ELBURZ MOUNTAINS

ZAGROS MOUNTAINS

Euphrates River

Tigris River

Mt Ararat

Salt Desert (Dasht-E Kavir)

Barren Desert (Dasht-E Lut)

Istanbul
Ankara
Nicosia
Beirut
Tel Aviv
Jerusalem
Amman
Damascus
Baghdad
Tabriz
Teheran
Isfahan
Mashad

Market
Carpet weaving
Watermelons
Tourism
Wild boar
Cherries
Brown bear
Tobacco
Whirling dervish
Cotton
Fox
Sheep
Goats
Dates
Clay houses
Wheat
Gas
Oil
Cotton
Wheat
Oil
Sheep
Barley
Cotton
Sturgeon
Tea
Rice
Making silk
Making clothes
Imam Mosque
Asiatic wild ass
Barley
Cotton
Dates
Wheat
Making clothes
Coffee
Limes
Lemons
Leopard
Dates
Wolf
Sailing
Oranges
Cruise ship

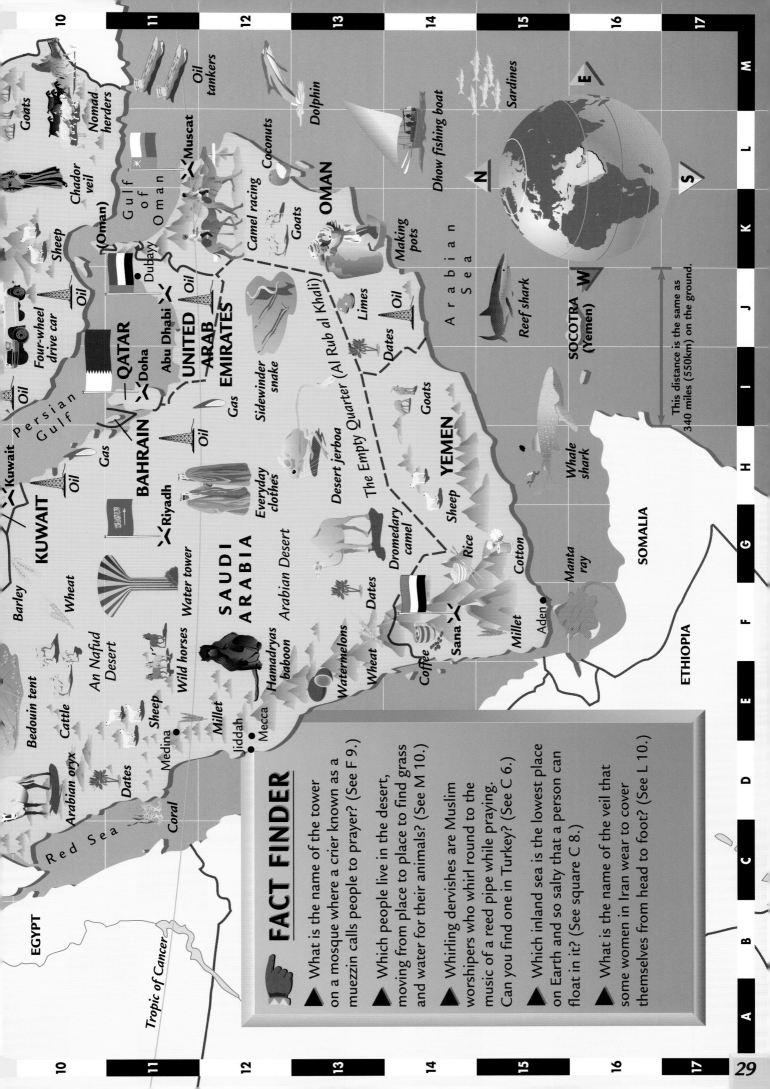

FACT FINDER

▲ What is the name of the tower on a mosque where a crier known as a muezzin calls people to prayer? (See F 9.)

▲ Which people live in the desert, moving from place to place to find grass and water for their animals? (See M 10.)

▲ Whirling dervishes are Muslim worshipers who whirl round to the music of a reed pipe while praying. Can you find one in Turkey? (See C 6.)

▲ Which inland sea is the lowest place on Earth and so salty that a person can float in it? (See square C 8.)

▲ What is the name of the veil that some women in Iran wear to cover themselves from head to foot? (See L 10.)

This distance is the same as 340 miles (550km) on the ground.

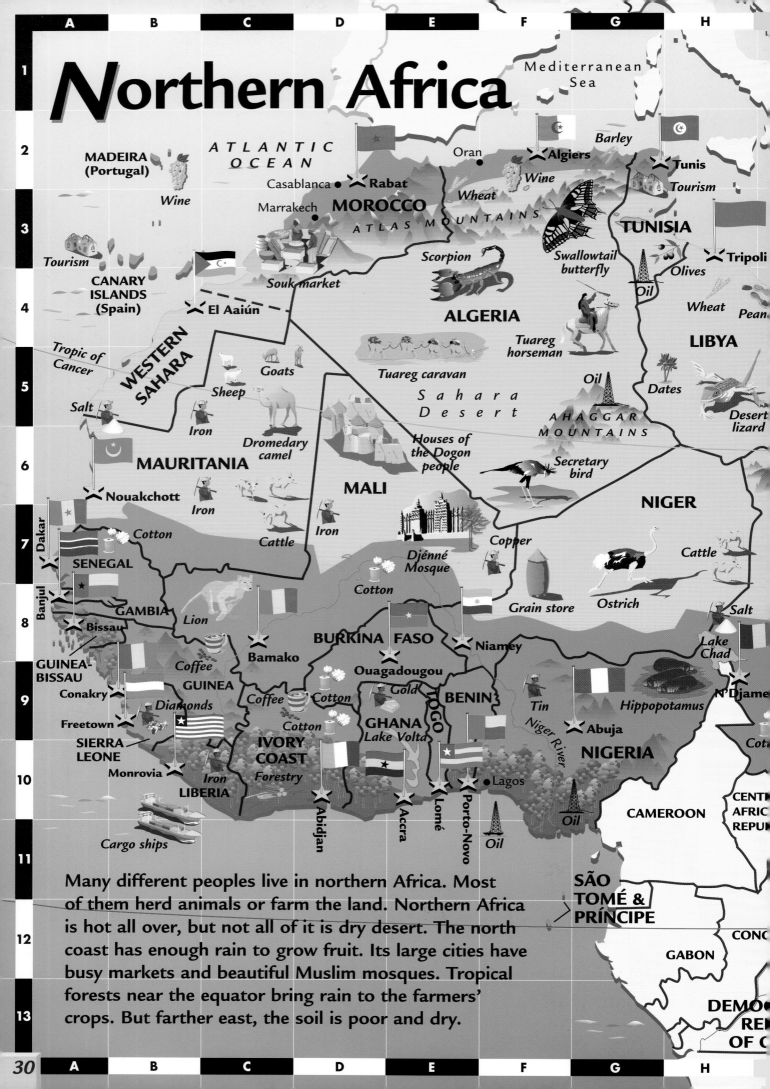

Northern Africa

Mediterranean Sea

ATLANTIC OCEAN

MADEIRA (Portugal)

Wine

Tourism

CANARY ISLANDS (Spain)

Tropic of Cancer

Salt

WESTERN SAHARA

✈ El Aaiún

MAURITANIA

✈ Nouakchott

Iron

Dakar

SENEGAL

Cotton

Banjul

GAMBIA

✈ Bissau

GUINEA-BISSAU

Conakry

Freetown

SIERRA LEONE

Monrovia

LIBERIA

Iron

Cargo ships

Lion

Diamonds

Coffee

GUINEA

Coffee

Cotton

IVORY COAST

Forestry

✈ Abidjan

Sheep

Goats

Iron

Dromedary camel

Cattle

Bamako

BURKINA FASO

✈ Ouagadougou

Cotton

Gold

GHANA

Lake Volta

✈ Accra

✈ Lomé

TOGO

Casablanca ● ✈ Rabat

Marrakech ●

MOROCCO

Souk market

ATLAS MOUNTAINS

Scorpion

Oran ●

✈ Algiers

Wine

Wheat

ALGERIA

Tuareg caravan

Sahara Desert

Houses of the Dogon people

MALI

Djénné Mosque

Cotton

Tuareg horseman

Copper

Grain store

AHAGGAR MOUNTAINS

Oil

Secretary bird

NIGER

✈ Niamey

Ostrich

BENIN

Tin

Hippopotamus

Niger River

✈ Abuja

NIGERIA

✈ Porto-Novo

● Lagos

Oil

Oil

Barley

✈ Algiers

Wine

TUNISIA

✈ Tunis

Tourism

✈ Tripoli

Olives

Oil

Wheat

Pean

LIBYA

Dates

Desert lizard

Cattle

Salt

Lake Chad

✈ N'Djame

CAMEROON

CENT AFRIC REPU

SÃO TOMÉ & PRÍNCIPE

GABON

CONG

DEMO RE OF C

Many different peoples live in northern Africa. Most of them herd animals or farm the land. Northern Africa is hot all over, but not all of it is dry desert. The north coast has enough rain to grow fruit. Its large cities have busy markets and beautiful Muslim mosques. Tropical forests near the equator bring rain to the farmers' crops. But farther east, the soil is poor and dry.

Swallowtail butterfly

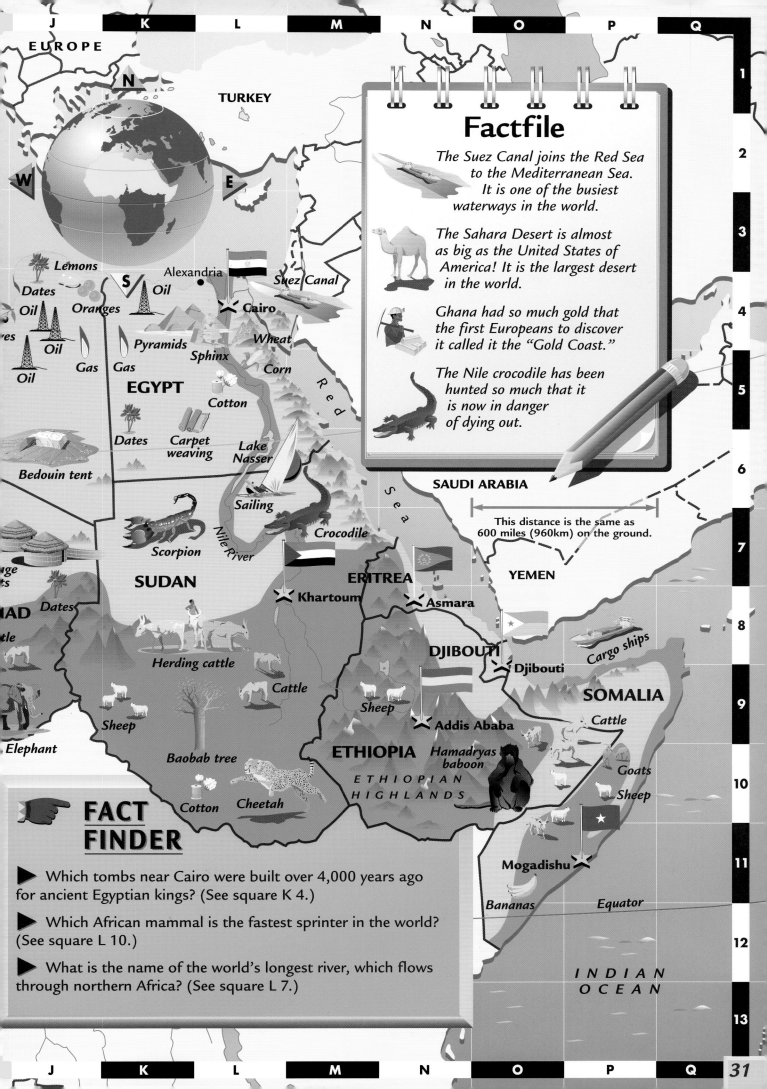

EUROPE

N

W — S — E

TURKEY

Factfile

The Suez Canal joins the Red Sea to the Mediterranean Sea. It is one of the busiest waterways in the world.

The Sahara Desert is almost as big as the United States of America! It is the largest desert in the world.

Ghana had so much gold that the first Europeans to discover it called it the "Gold Coast."

The Nile crocodile has been hunted so much that it is now in danger of dying out.

Lemons

Dates

Oil

Oranges

Oil

Alexandria

Oil

Cairo

Suez Canal

Pyramids

Wheat

Sphinx

Corn

Gas   Gas

EGYPT

Cotton

Dates

Carpet weaving

Lake Nasser

Bedouin tent

Sailing

Nile River

SAUDI ARABIA

This distance is the same as 600 miles (960km) on the ground.

Red Sea

Scorpion

Crocodile

SUDAN

Khartoum

ERITREA

Asmara

YEMEN

HAD

Dates

ttle

Herding cattle

Cattle

Sheep

DJIBOUTI

Djibouti

Cargo ships

SOMALIA

Cattle

Sheep

Elephant

Baobab tree

ETHIOPIA

Hamadryas baboon

Addis Ababa

Goats

Sheep

Cotton

Cheetah

ETHIOPIAN HIGHLANDS

Mogadishu

FACT FINDER

▶ Which tombs near Cairo were built over 4,000 years ago for ancient Egyptian kings? (See square K 4.)

▶ Which African mammal is the fastest sprinter in the world? (See square L 10.)

▶ What is the name of the world's longest river, which flows through northern Africa? (See square L 7.)

Bananas

Equator

INDIAN OCEAN

1
2
3
4
5
6
7
8
9
10
11
12
13

Southern Africa

Southern Africa is a vast land of grasslands, rain forests, mountains, and deserts. The plains of Kenya and Tanzania are famous for their huge herds of animals. Farther west, in the rain forests, there are gorillas, monkeys, and tropical birds. Many different peoples live in Africa. Most of them farm in small villages, but the cities are growing. Many countries mine copper and gold. Some mine diamonds too.

Factfile

Southern Africa is home to the black rhino and the mountain gorilla, two of the world's most endangered animals.

Southern Africa has large areas of rain forest. Altogether, nearly one-quarter of the world's forests grow in southern Africa.

Three-quarters of the world's diamonds are mined in southern Africa.

This distance is the same as 450 miles (725km) on the ground.

Tropic of Cancer

Equator

N
W
S
E

SEYCHELLES

NIGERIA

Yams

Coffee

Forestry
Oil
Yaoundé
CAMEROON
Malabo
EQUATORIAL
GUINEA
Oil

Forestry
Libreville
GABON
Oil

CHAD

CENTRAL AFRICAN REPUBLIC

Cassava

Yams

Cotton

Forestry
Bangui
Diamonds

Forestry
Brazzaville
CONGO
Kinshasa
CABINDA
(Angola)
Oil

Crocodile

Okapi

Dug-out
canoes

Forestry

Kasai River

Cassava

DEMOCRATIC
REPUBLIC
OF CONGO

Diamonds

Congo River

Chimpanzee

Mountain
gorilla

Coffee

Coffee

SUDAN

ETHIOPIA

SOMALIA

Flamingos

KENYA

Office
blocks

Nairobi

Tea

Coffee

Kampala
UGANDA

Lake
Victoria

R

Kigali
RWANDA
Bujumbura
BURUNDI

Lake
Tanganyika

Mt. Kilimanjaro

Elephants

Tourism

Zanzibar
Island

Dodoma

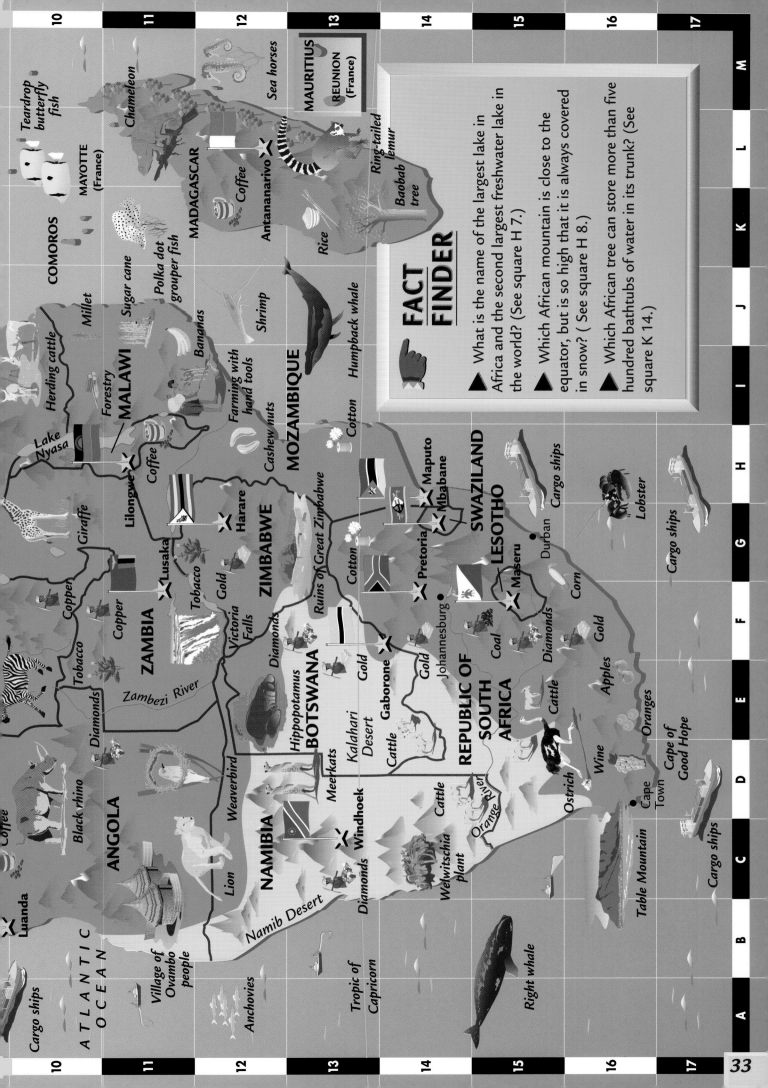

Southern Asia

Southern Asia stretches from the Himalaya in the north of India to the island of Sri Lanka in the south. The weather is mostly hot and dry, although for several months of the year there are heavy rains. More than a billion people live in southern Asia. Most people live in villages and farm the land, but many are beginning to move to the cities. The cities are a mixture of old and new, with modern buildings next to ancient temples and palaces. The busy streets are packed with cars, trucks and buses, but also with bullock-carts and elephants.

👉 FACT FINDER

▲ Which white marble temple, decorated with precious stones, was built in the 17th century by an Indian emperor as a burial place for his wife? (See square G 8.)

▲ In India, which animal is used to help people with heavy work such as moving timber? (See square F 11.)

▲ What are Pakistan, Afghanistan, and India all famous for weaving? (See squares C 6, C 9 and F 7.)

▲ In India, which three-wheeled vehicle that looks a little like a bicycle is often used to carry people from one place to another? (See square I 10.)

TURKMENISTAN

UZBEKISTAN

TAJIKISTAN

CHINA

AFGHANISTAN

Bactrian camel

Milking goats

Cotton

Cattle

Blue Mosque

Carpet weaving

Kabul

Rubies

Helmand River

Peaches

Goats

Wheat

Quetta

PAKISTAN

Wheat

Cotton

Wheat

Cobra

Indus River

Sugar cane

Cattle

Shah Faisal Mosque

Islamabad

Lahore

KARAKORAM

Carpet weaving

Wheat

Goats

New Delhi

Snow leopard

RANGE

Yak

Mountain peaks

Mt. Everest

HIMALAYA

NEPAL

Kathmandu

Sugar

Tea

BHUTAN

Thimphu

Brahmaputra River

Indian rhino

Tea

Oil

Buddhist monk

Factfile

More films are made in southern Asia than anywhere else in the world. India makes over 800 films a year.

The mountains of southern Asia are home to the snow leopard, one of the world's most endangered animals.

Southern Asia is the world's largest producer of tea.

This distance is the same as 360 miles (575km) on the ground.

MYANMAR

BANGLADESH

INDIA

SRI LANKA

MALDIVE ISLANDS

ANDAMAN ISLANDS (India)

NICOBAR ISLANDS (India)

INDIAN OCEAN

Equator

Tropic of Cancer

VINHDAYA RANGE

Narmada River

Godavari River

Karachi
Ahmadabad
Nagpur
Bombay
Hyderabad
Bangalore
Madras
Cochin
Colombo
Calcutta
Chittagong
Vishakhapatnam

Film making
Wheat
Sheep
Dromedary camels
Peanuts
Cotton
Oil
Making clothes
Steam train
Tourism
Film making
Peacock
Forestry
Coal
Working elephant
Black bear
Bicycle rickshaw
Rice
Coal
Rice
Iron
Crocodile
Making silk
Car building
Water buffalo
Classical Indian dancing
Black panther
Cotton
Millet
Iron
Gold
Goods truck
Car building
Tiger
Cattle
Rice
Coconuts
Tea
Ship building
Shrimp
Coral
Scuba diving
Clown fish
Outrigger fishing boat
Sardines
Pearls
Car building

weaving
Herring
Dhow fishing boat
Blue whale
Lobster
Reef shark
Dolphins
Humpback whale
Polka dot grouper fish
Coral

N
W E
S

35

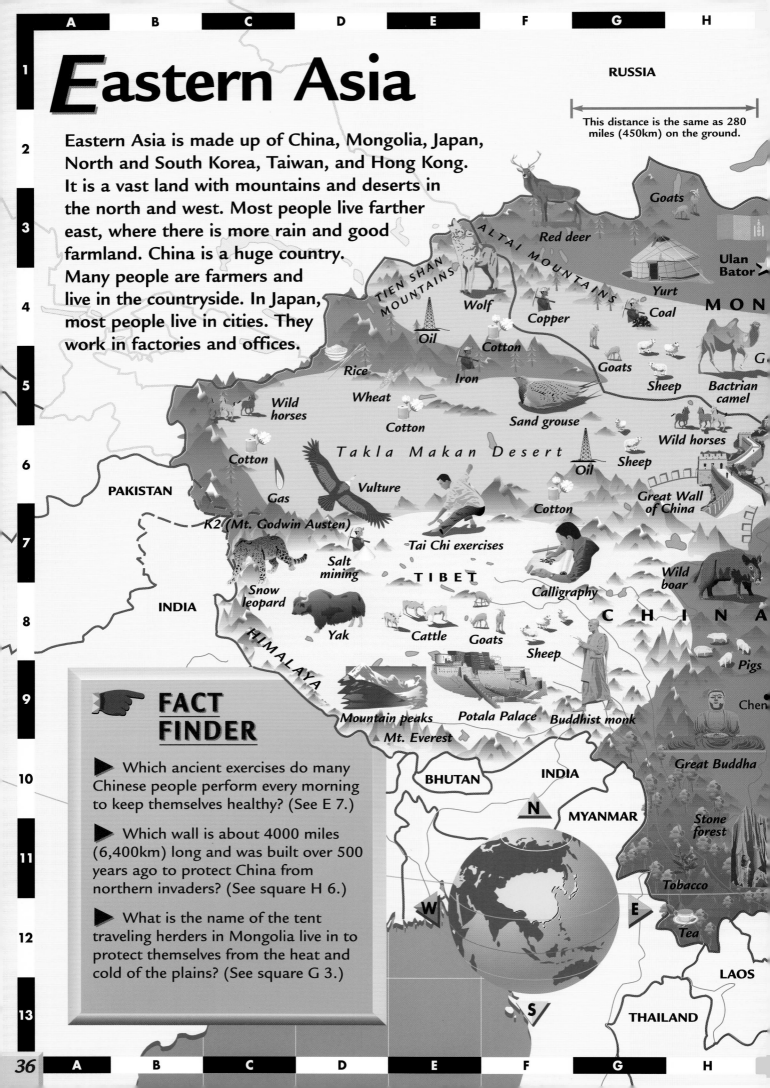

Eastern Asia

Eastern Asia is made up of China, Mongolia, Japan, North and South Korea, Taiwan, and Hong Kong. It is a vast land with mountains and deserts in the north and west. Most people live farther east, where there is more rain and good farmland. China is a huge country. Many people are farmers and live in the countryside. In Japan, most people live in cities. They work in factories and offices.

This distance is the same as 280 miles (450km) on the ground.

RUSSIA

Goats
Red deer
ALTAI MOUNTAINS
Yurt
Ulan Bator
Coal
M O N
TIEN SHAN MOUNTAINS
Wolf
Copper
G
Oil
Cotton
Goats
Rice
Iron
Sheep
Bactrian camel
Wheat
Cotton
Sand grouse
Wild horses
Wild horses
Takla Makan Desert
Cotton
Oil
Sheep
Cotton
Great Wall of China
PAKISTAN
Gas
Vulture
K2 (Mt. Godwin Austen)
Tai Chi exercises
Wild boar
Salt mining
TIBET
Calligraphy
C H I N A
Snow leopard
INDIA
Yak
Cattle
Goats
Sheep
Pigs
HIMALAYA
Mountain peaks
Potala Palace
Buddhist monk
Chen
Mt. Everest
Great Buddha
BHUTAN
INDIA
N
MYANMAR
Stone forest
Tobacco
E
W
LAOS
Tea
S
THAILAND

FACT FINDER

▶ Which ancient exercises do many Chinese people perform every morning to keep themselves healthy? (See E 7.)

▶ Which wall is about 4000 miles (6,400km) long and was built over 500 years ago to protect China from northern invaders? (See square H 6.)

▶ What is the name of the tent traveling herders in Mongolia live in to protect themselves from the heat and cold of the plains? (See square G 3.)

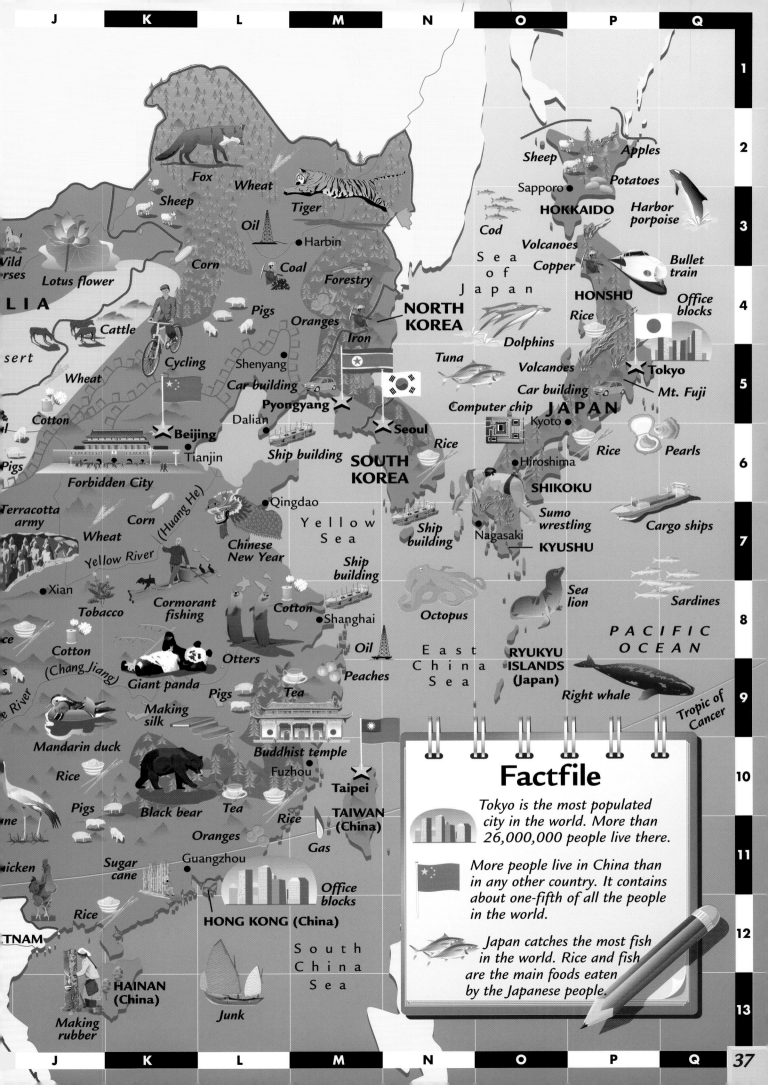

Factfile

Tokyo is the most populated city in the world. More than 26,000,000 people live there.

More people live in China than in any other country. It contains about one-fifth of all the people in the world.

Japan catches the most fish in the world. Rice and fish are the main foods eaten by the Japanese people.

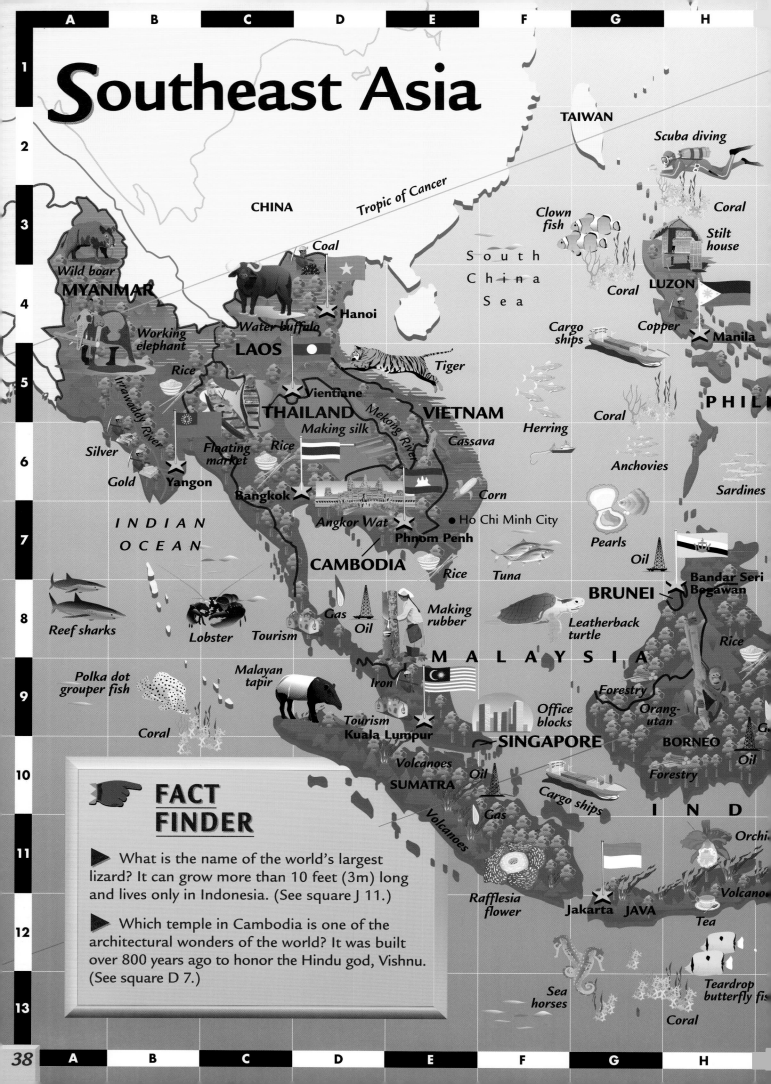

Southeast Asia

TAIWAN

CHINA

Tropic of Cancer

Scuba diving

Coral

Clown fish

Stilt house

Coal

S o u t h

C h i n a

S e a

LUZON

Wild boar

MYANMAR

Coral

Working elephant

Hanoi

Cargo ships

Copper

Manila

Water buffalo

Rice

LAOS

Tiger

P H I L I

Irrawaddy River

Silver

Vientiane

Herring

Coral

Making silk

THAILAND

VIETNAM

Cassava

Anchovies

Gold

Yangon

Floating market

Rice

Corn

Sardines

Bangkok

Ho Chi Minh City

Pearls

I N D I A N

O C E A N

Angkor Wat

Phnom Penh

Rice

Tuna

Oil

BRUNEI

CAMBODIA

Bandar Seri Begawan

Reef sharks

Lobster

Gas

Oil

Making rubber

Leatherback turtle

M A L A Y S I A

Rice

Tourism

Polka dot grouper fish

Malayan tapir

Iron

Forestry

Orang-utan

Coral

Tourism

Kuala Lumpur

Office blocks

SINGAPORE

BORNEO

Oil

I N D

Volcanoes

SUMATRA

Oil

Cargo ships

Forestry

Orchi

FACT FINDER

► What is the name of the world's largest lizard? It can grow more than 10 feet (3m) long and lives only in Indonesia. (See square J 11.)

► Which temple in Cambodia is one of the architectural wonders of the world? It was built over 800 years ago to honor the Hindu god, Vishnu. (See square D 7.)

Gas

Volcanoes

Rafflesia flower

Jakarta **JAVA**

Volcano

Tea

Sea horses

Teardrop butterfly fis

Coral

Southeast Asia is made up of a narrow
strip of land and thousands of small
islands. The area has high mountains,
tropical forests, and river valleys. The
weather is hot and wet all year round.
Many of the people are farmers, who
grow rice and corn for food, and
rubber and coffee to sell. But the cities
are growing, and more people are
finding work in factories and offices.

Factfile

Rubber is made from the sap of
the rubber tree. Southeast Asia
produces over three-quarters of
the world's rubber.

There are more active volcanoes
in southeast Asia than in any
other area of the world. The
ash left behind from volcanic
eruptions helps to make the soil
good for farming.

The country of Indonesia is made
up of over 13,600 islands. It is the
biggest chain of islands in the
world and has the world's
fourth largest population.

This distance is the same as
500 miles (800km) on the ground.

Bicycle
rickshaw

N E S

Coconuts

MINDANAO

Outrigger fishing boat

N O R T H

P A C I F I C

O C E A N

Equator

Tuna

Bird of
paradise

Coconuts

Sponge

Gas   Oil

**IRIAN JAYA
(Indonesia)**

conuts

MALUKU

**PAPUA NEW
GUINEA**

Shrimp

Bananas

Cloves

Tree
kangaroo

Echidna

Port Moresby

SULAWESI

Flying
lizard

Crab

Humpback
whale

Coffee

E   S   I   A

Manta
ray

modo
agon

FLORES

TIMOR

LI

SUMBA

Shrimp

urism

AUSTRALIA

Dolphins

Tropic of
Capricorn

Australia, New Zealand, and the Pacific Islands

The Pacific Ocean is dotted with thousands of islands. Many people live in villages and grow crops or hunt for fish. Australia is an island too, but it is so big that it is a continent. Most Australians live in cities or farm land near the coast. A lot of Australia is hot and dry, but it has mountains and rain forests too. It also has animals and plants that are not found anywhere else.

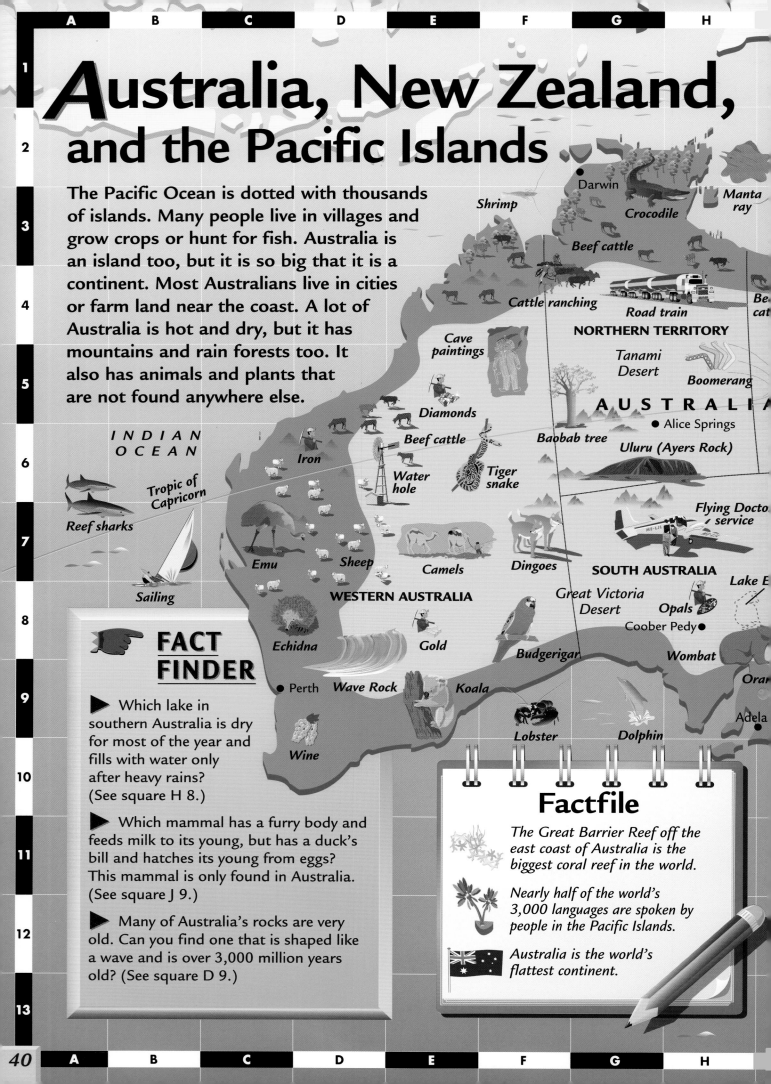

Darwin

Shrimp

Crocodile

Manta ray

Beef cattle

Cattle ranching

Road train

NORTHERN TERRITORY

Bee catt

Cave paintings

Tanami Desert

Boomerang

INDIAN OCEAN

Diamonds

Beef cattle

AUSTRALIA

Baobab tree

Alice Springs

Uluru (Ayers Rock)

Iron

Water hole

Tiger snake

Tropic of Capricorn

Reef sharks

Flying Docto service

Camels

Dingoes

SOUTH AUSTRALIA

Lake E

Sailing

Emu

Sheep

WESTERN AUSTRALIA

Great Victoria Desert

Opals

Coober Pedy

Wombat

Echidna

Gold

Budgerigar

Orar

Perth

Wave Rock

Koala

Adela

Lobster

Dolphin

Wine

FACT FINDER

► Which lake in southern Australia is dry for most of the year and fills with water only after heavy rains? (See square H 8.)

► Which mammal has a furry body and feeds milk to its young, but has a duck's bill and hatches its young from eggs? This mammal is only found in Australia. (See square J 9.)

► Many of Australia's rocks are very old. Can you find one that is shaped like a wave and is over 3,000 million years old? (See square D 9.)

Factfile

The Great Barrier Reef off the east coast of Australia is the biggest coral reef in the world.

Nearly half of the world's 3,000 languages are spoken by people in the Pacific Islands.

Australia is the world's flattest continent.

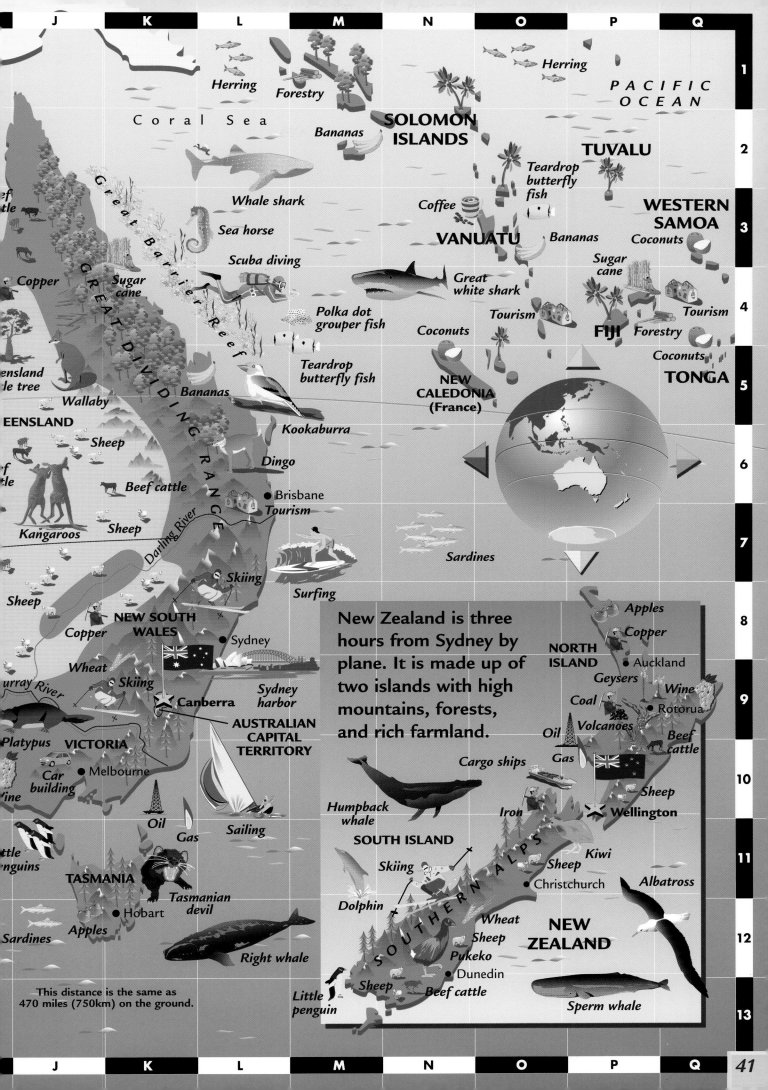

PACIFIC OCEAN

Herring

Herring

Forestry

Coral Sea

Bananas

SOLOMON ISLANDS

TUVALU

Teardrop butterfly fish

Coffee

WESTERN SAMOA

Whale shark

Coconuts

Sea horse

VANUATU

Bananas

Sugar cane

Scuba diving

Great white shark

Tourism

Copper

Sugar cane

Coconuts

Tourism

FIJI

Forestry

Polka dot grouper fish

Coconuts

ef tle

Teardrop butterfly fish

NEW CALEDONIA (France)

Coconuts

TONGA

ensland le tree

Bananas

Wallaby

EENSLAND

Kookaburra

Sheep

Dingo

Beef cattle

● Brisbane

Tourism

Kangaroos

Sheep

Sardines

Sheep

Skiing

Apples

Surfing

Copper

NORTH ISLAND

● Auckland

Copper

Wheat

NEW SOUTH WALES

Geysers

Wine

Skiing

● Sydney

Coal

● Rotorua

rray River

Sydney harbor

Canberra

Volcanoes

Oil

Beef cattle

Platypus

VICTORIA

AUSTRALIAN CAPITAL TERRITORY

New Zealand is three hours from Sydney by plane. It is made up of two islands with high mountains, forests, and rich farmland.

Gas

ine

Car building

● Melbourne

Cargo ships

Sheep

Wellington

Oil

Gas

Sailing

Iron

ttle nguins

Humpback whale

SOUTH ISLAND

Kiwi

Sheep

Albatross

TASMANIA

Skiing

Sheep

● Christchurch

Sardines

Tasmanian devil

Dolphin

Wheat

Apples

● Hobart

Sheep

NEW ZEALAND

Pukeko

Right whale

Sheep

● Dunedin

Beef cattle

This distance is the same as 470 miles (750km) on the ground.

Little penguin

Little penguin

Sperm whale

Fascinating facts

On these pages, you can discover interesting facts about the world. Look up the names of the places in the index and find out where they are on the maps in this atlas.

Where in the world is...

...the hottest place?
Al Aziziyah in Libya. The highest temperature ever recorded was 136°F (58°C).

In Al Aziziyah, you could fry an egg on a sun-baked rock.

...the coldest place?
Vostock in Antarctica. The lowest temperature ever recorded was -129°F. (-89°C). This is over three times as cold as inside a deep freeze.

...the wettest place?
Mawsynram in India, where nearly 40 feet (12m) of rain falls each year. This is enough to cover a three-story building.

...the driest place?
Atacama Desert in Chile, where it has rained only a few times in the last 400 years.

Which country is the...

...biggest country?
Russia, which is 6,592,850 square miles (17,075,400sq km).

...smallest country?
Vatican City, which is 109 acres (44 hectares).

If Russia were the size of a soccer field, the Vatican City would be the size of a small stamp.

...emptiest country?
Mongolia, which has a huge desert and towering mountains. There are only a few towns which are far apart.

...most crowded country?
Monaco, which is a tiny country in Europe. It has an orchestra larger than its army.

Where is the...

...highest mountain in the world?
Mount Everest in the Himalaya, in Nepal. It is about 29,028 ft. (8,848m) high—over nine times as tall as the highest waterfall in the world.

29,028 feet

...highest waterfall in the world?
Angel Falls, in Venezuela. It has a total drop of about 3,212 ft. (979m)—over twice as high as the tallest building in North America.

3,212 feet

...highest geyser in the world?
Waimangu Geyser, in New Zealand. It once shot out a jet of water 1,510 ft. (460m) high—slightly taller than Sears Tower.

1,510 feet

...highest building in North America?
Sears Tower, US. It is about 1,454 ft. (443m) tall—nearly four times taller than the tallest tree in the world.

1,454 feet

...highest tree in the world?
A redwood tree in California, US. It is about 368 ft. (112m) high—over 40 times taller than the tallest person in the world.

368 feet

Who was the world's tallest person?
An American called Robert Pershing Wadlow was the world's tallest person. He was over 8 ft., 11 in. (2.7m) tall.

FACT FINDER

Find these record-breaking places in the atla

▶ The highest mountain (page 34, square J

▶ The tallest waterfall (page 20, square E 4

▶ The longest river (page 31, square L 7)

▶ The driest place (page 21, square E 9)

42

W

E

• London

• New York

• Tokyo

What time is it?

Across the world, at the same moment, clocks show different times. This is because the world is divided into time zones. All time is measured from Greenwich, London, UK. When you cross a time zone to the east of Greenwich, time is one hour ahead. When you cross a time zone to the west of Greenwich, time is one hour behind.

The letters *am* stand for ante meridian, which means the hours from midnight until mid-day, or the morning. The letters *pm* stand for post meridian, which means the hours from mid-day until midnight, or the afternoon and evening.

If it is 12pm in London, what time is it in New York and Tokyo?

Land and sea

Imagine the world as a cake. Most of the cake would be oceans and seas, and one small slice would be the land. Most of the slice of land would be desert, rain forest, mountains, ice and grassland. Less than half the slice would be places where people can live and farm. In this atlas, you can find the biggest rain forest on page 20, see square H 5, and the biggest desert on page 30, see square E 5.

Which are the three longest rivers?

The Nile River in North Africa is 4,145 miles (6,671km) long. You could walk along its length in over four months.

The Amazon River in South America is 4,000 miles (6,437km) long. You could run along its length in over two months.

The Yangtze River in China is 3,915 miles (6,300km) long. You could cycle fast from one end to the other in just over one month.

Index

This index lists all the places on the maps in this atlas. The page number tells you which map to go to and the grid reference tells you where the place is on the map. You can find out how to use grid references on page 9.

*T*roubleshooting tips

System requirements

The Atlas disc will work on most Windows or Apple Macintosh computers.
To check that it will run on yours, please read the minimum specifications below.

- **Windows**
  486DX/33Mhz PC with Windows version 3.1, 3.11, 95 (or later); SVGA color monitor; Soundblaster-compatible soundcard; 8Mb RAM (16Mb RAM recommended with Windows 95)

- **Macintosh**
  Apple Macintosh with 68020 processor (or greater), system 7.0 (or later) and 8Mb of RAM.

Quick fixes

To get the most out of your Atlas disc, please check:
1. Your monitor is set to 640 x 480 and 256 colors.
2. You have the Arial font (Windows users) or Helvetica font (Macintosh users) installed in your fonts folder.
3. You have no other applications open.

Read me file

If you have a problem with your Atlas disk that is not covered in the notes above, be sure to check the Read me file. You can open the Read me file by clicking on the Read me icon that you will find next to the Atlas icon.

Helpline

If you come across a problem loading or running the Atlas disc, you should find the solution here. If you still cannot solve your problem, call the helpline at 1-800-424-1280.

Published in the United States by
World Book, Inc.
525 W. Monroe
20th Floor
Chicago, IL 60661
in association with Two-Can Publishing Ltd.

Disc
Creative Director: Jason Page
Programming Director: Paul Steven
Art Director: Sarah Evans
Senior Designer: James Evans
Editors: Rob Mitchell, Lyndall Thomas
Programmer: Roger Emery
Authors: Jason Page, Rob Mitchell,
Lyndall Thomas, Lucy Arnold
Illustrators: Jon Stuart, James Jarvis,
Mel Pickering
Production Director: Lorraine Estelle
Project Manager: Joya Bart-Plange
U.S. Editor: Melissa Tucker, World Book
Publishing

Book
Text: Andrew Solway
Consultant: Steve Watts
Computer Illustrations: Mel Pickering,
Jacqueline Land
Editors: Deborah Kespert, Kate Asser,
Editorial Support: Claire Llewellyn,
Julia Hillyard, Claire Yude
Art Director: Belinda Webster
Senior Designer: Helen Holmes
Designer: Michele Egar

**For information on other World Book
products, call 1-800-255-1750, ext. 2238, or
visit us at our Website at
http://www.worldbook.com**

ISBN: 0-7166-9910-9

Printed in Hong Kong

1 2 3 4 5 6 7 8 9 10 02 01 99 98

CHECK OUT ALL THE INTERFACT TITLES

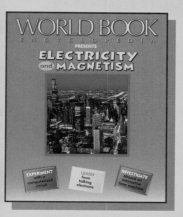

WORLD BOOK ENCYCLOPEDIA PRESENTS
ELECTRICITY and MAGNETISM

CD (PC/MAC) ISBN 0-7166-7209-X

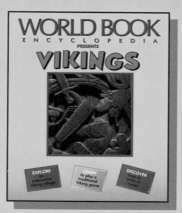

WORLD BOOK ENCYCLOPEDIA PRESENTS
VIKINGS

CD (PC/MAC) ISBN 0-7166-7221-9

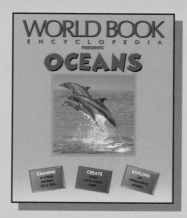

WORLD BOOK ENCYCLOPEDIA PRESENTS
OCEANS

CD (PC/MAC) ISBN 0-7166-7212-X

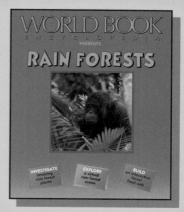

WORLD BOOK ENCYCLOPEDIA PRESENTS
RAIN FORESTS

CD (PC/MAC) ISBN 0-7166-7230-8

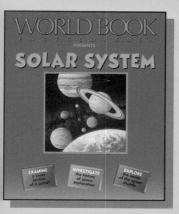

WORLD BOOK ENCYCLOPEDIA PRESENTS
SOLAR SYSTEM

CD (PC/MAC) ISBN 0-7166-7218-9

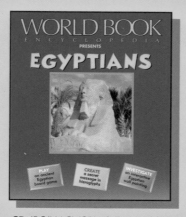

WORLD BOOK ENCYCLOPEDIA PRESENTS
EGYPTIANS

CD (PC/MAC) ISBN 0-7166-7206-5

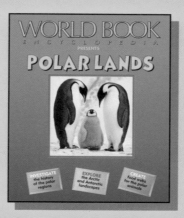

WORLD BOOK ENCYCLOPEDIA PRESENTS
POLAR LANDS

CD (PC/MAC) ISBN 0-7166-7227-8

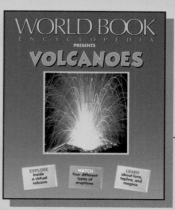

WORLD BOOK ENCYCLOPEDIA PRESENTS
VOLCANOES

CD (PC/MAC) ISBN 0-7166-7224-3

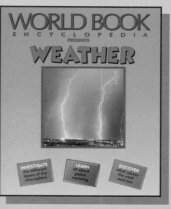

WORLD BOOK ENCYCLOPEDIA PRESENTS
WEATHER

CD (PC/MAC) ISBN 0-7166-7236-7

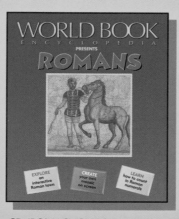

WORLD BOOK ENCYCLOPEDIA PRESENTS
ROMANS

CD (PC/MAC) ISBN 0-7166-7215-4

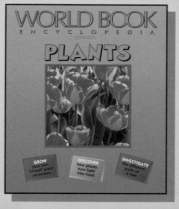

WORLD BOOK ENCYCLOPEDIA PRESENTS
PLANTS

CD (PC/MAC) ISBN 0-7166-7239-1

WORLD BOOK ENCYCLOPEDIA PRESENTS
AZTECS

CD (PC/MAC) ISBN 0-7166-7250-2

WORLD BOOK ENCYCLOPEDIA PRESENTS
SENSES

CD (PC/MAC) ISBN 0-7166-7233-2

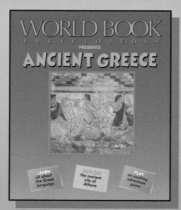

WORLD BOOK ENCYCLOPEDIA PRESENTS
ANCIENT GREECE

CD (PC/MAC) ISBN 0-7166-7234-0

There is an increasing number of
INTERFACT titles to choose from.

Ask your retailer to show
you them or order them for you.